Moving In

Ten Successful Independent/Transitional Living Programs

Edited by Mark J. Kroner, MSW, LSW

Published by Northwest Media, Inc., Eugene, Oregon

Moving In Ten Successful Independent/Transitional Living Programs

Published by:

Northwest Media, Inc. ■ 326 West 12th Avenue ■ Eugene, Oregon 97401
phone: 541-343-6636/fax: 541-343-0177
e-mail: nwm@northwestmedia.com
Web address: www.northwestmedia.com

Illustrations and design by Diane Cissel

Printed in the United States of America
ISBN 1-892194-24-4

Contents

Foreword

Like all truly valued books in the field, this book shares the knowledge and experience of those who have it with those who want to listen. Our goal was to have a frank comparison of successful transitional living projects for all to review. Accordingly, the answers that appear in each chapter were guided by the same set of questions sent to writers from selected agencies.

We chose to let each chapter stand alone, in the words of its contributor. This gives you the option of reading the book as a collection of model programs, or as a way of gaining insight into those programs through the voices and attitudes of the staff as they recount their successes and failures.

Although not all the contributors followed the question list line by line, readers can visit the chapters and filter out answers to particular questions. For example, if you are interested in housing options, you can directly compare answers across programs by scanning each chapter for that question.

This book represents a love for the idea of Transitional Living and a deep desire to help agencies and their dedicated staff to help youth in transition. Mark Kroner and Carol Nelson were the glue that held this project together. Mark, from start to finish, made the book happen. His commitment to the field was recognized last year when he received the National Independent Living Association Founders' Award. I know that his greatest rewards are in his heart for his many years of service. Thank you, Mark. And thanks to Carol and all the contributing writers who volunteered their time to share their experiences.

Lee White
President, Northwest Media, Inc.
January 1, 2001

Introduction

Mark J. Kroner, MSW, LSW

If you are interested in this book, you have undoubtedly already made the connection between independent living preparation and a young person's need for actual firsthand experience at living independently. Participating in an independent living program without an actual housing experience is like taking driver's training without a car. Even the best life skills training programs will not be fully effective without giving youth the chance to put the skills to use in real-world settings.

Since I began working in the independent living field in 1986, hundreds of independent and transitional living programs have been developed around the country. If you are new to this field, you will soon discover that the terms "independent living" and "transitional living" are used interchangeably. (Many providers would like to replace both terms with "self-sufficiency preparation," since virtually no one is ever truly independent.) In general, independent living (IL) programs work with youth in state or county custody, while transitional living (TL) programs assist non-systems, homeless young adults. However, this is not always the case, and the reader is advised to find out what the terms mean to the person using them. This book includes chapters about IL programs, TL programs, and combined IL-TL programs. All of them are trying less-supervised living arrangements than usually provided in traditional out-of-home placements. This is an important new development in the child welfare field. Unfortunately, most IL and TL programs in the country do not venture far beyond life skills training and support services. We hope this book will stimulate new ideas and give providers a clear picture of how they can develop their own programs.

The passage of the Foster Care Independence Act of 1999 has helped service providers focus on the realities of older youth unable to live at home and their need for accessible and affordable housing, giving states the option of using up to 30% of the new funding for housing. States and agencies new to this area of service can learn from the experiences of others. This book explores the positive and negative aspects of ten programs that are "fighting the good fight" in order to develop what the youth and young adults in their care need to succeed. Each program has something unique to offer the reader. The writers average over 8 years each in the IL field.

We worked hard to find and include a diverse selection of programs. All of them provide their participants with the valuable experience of living independently in addition to life skills training. Some, like Lighthouse in Ohio and Kenosha in Wisconsin, have been up and running for over a decade, with hundreds of success (and many "less than success") stories. While most are private organizations, Franklin County Children Services in Ohio provides a successful model of a publicly operated housing-based ILP. Youth Continuum in New Haven, Connecticut is an example of a successful model that includes both IL and TL programs and sources of funding. Some of the programs are funded solely by Federal Transitional Living Grants, while others receive per diems from their states or counties. Programs such as Green Chimneys in New York City (for gay, lesbian, bisexual, transgendered, and questioning youth) and the Latin American Youth Center in Washington, D.C. developed out of an awareness of the need to combine IL preparation with cultural realities for certain client groups. Most of the programs are in urban settings. However, Quakerdale in Iowa and the Spectrum program in Vermont exist in small to medium-sized towns. The Nevada project has a focus on youth in the correctional system, and Open-Inn in Tucson demonstrates how multiple funding sources can create a comprehensive program serving a wide age range.

Despite the many differences between them, all of the programs included in this book have something crucial in common: the persistence of a small group of dedicated professionals who did whatever it took to make sure that the youth in their communities didn't leave the system without at least a chance to learn what it takes to survive as a responsible adult. Their success rates are never 100%, but all consider their programs to be ever improving works in progress and seriously wish they could reach more youth.

We hope this book will motivate the reader to develop a "we can do this!" mind set. Most assuredly, one will finish the book with many new questions on how to make it work in one's own neck of the woods. Each author could have easily written a whole book on the experiences of his or her program, but we had to stop somewhere!

There will always be youth and young adults who need outside help in making the transition to adulthood. There is probably no group in society more vulnerable than older youth without any stable family support. It is our job to make them less vulnerable, and it is our belief that providing them with actual independent living experience prior to emancipation is a potentially powerful way of doing that job.

Best of luck in your efforts to develop new housing options in your community!

1

Spectrum Youth & Family Services
Transitional Community-Based Living Program

Burlington, Vermont
Jackie Smith

Brief History

Spectrum's Transitional Community-Based Living Program (CBL) first opened its doors in 1988, in response to a request by the Department of Education. From that time, CBL has grown in its efforts toward meeting the needs of systems youth in Vermont requiring independent living services. Currently, Vermont youth leaving state care have few options for learning life skills. The CBL program offers five living options through which teens can begin their journey to self-sufficiency prior to aging out of custody.

Over the past few years, the collaboration between the Departments of Education, Mental Health, Corrections, and Social and Rehabilitative Services has grown stronger and more inclusive. A creative approach to services allows all qualified youth to be served. Many of the teens leaving our programs become responsible citizens of their communities.

Spectrum Youth and Family Services offers a variety of independent living services from which teens may enter the CBL program. Spectrum is increasingly responsive to the needs of the young people in its community. Its primary aim is to teach youth valuable life skills to prepare them for their transition to independent living.

Description of the Program

CBL Program Objectives

The objectives of the CBL program are two-fold:

1. Offer all teens the opportunity to gain self-sufficiency skills.

2. Allow youth the opportunity to fail while providing support and guidance.

Spectrum believes that gaining independent living skills is critical and that these skills must be acquired during a very challenging time in a teen's life.

Types of Housing Options Utilized

We offer five living options that can be modified for each youth wanting to access services.

■ The first option within the CBL continuum is our **foster care** option. This program serves youth between the ages of 9-18 years. We currently have a variety of homes within a three-county vicinity of our Burlington office. These homes are staffed by adults in different family situations: married couples with and without children, single people, single parents with children, and people residing with a live-in partner. We believe that this open approach best meets the needs of the young people utilizing our services. All foster parents are screened and licensed. They are required to receive monthly trainings and weekly (if not more frequent) case-management sessions. We offer all foster parents and recipients of our services access to a crisis line should consultation be requested.

■ The next most supervised living situation is our **wraparound program**, which provides two living options, Levels I (less intensive) and II (more intensive). This program is especially designed to meet the more challenging behaviors displayed by some youth while still providing them with access to skill acquisition. The program is open to males and females between the ages of 16 and 21 years. Teens are placed in Level I or II of the program, based on a thorough assessment and group interview process with the CBL unit. Decisions are very much team driven. Members of the unit believe that they all play a role in a teen's success in CBL. Teens entering the wrap program receive a higher level of supervision and often a greater therapeutic component than their counterparts in our other living options. Typically the teen lives with a wrap mentor in the community and reports to the mentor much like a residential staff. As teens gain skills, they engage in a step-down approach designed to assist them in transitioning to the next living option.

When a teen enters our program, a discharge plan is developed to help guide the treatment team in the provision of services. An average length of stay in the wrap program is 1 year. While in program, goals are developed and addressed in weekly case management meetings with the wrap mentor and case manager.

- The option at the next level in our continuum is our **mentor program**. This unique living option was developed 10 years ago and continues to grow and change in response to the needs of the population being served. The mentor program is open to kids between the ages of 16-21 years. All teens are required to go through a living assessment in Phase One of the program and a formal group interview. A case manager develops program

Client Comment

"This program gave me the chance to show people I could be independent....I knew I had the skills!"

goals and helps in the process of finding a mentor with whom the teen can live. The mentor's responsibility in this program is less extensive than that of the wrap mentor. Here, the mentor is a healthy, positive roommate who can provide guidance to a teen. The mentor is required to attend a weekly meeting with a case manager, as well as a weekly meeting between the teen and case manager. The teen will also meet once a week with his or her case manager to process goals and issues that have arisen throughout the week.

Each teen in any of our housing options is required to set both long- and short-term goals. In the mentor program, teens receive a weekly stipend. The amount of the stipend depends on the completion of goals, but is never less than $20 or in excess of $45. The stipend is budgeted to cover food, utilities, and rent. All the utilities are placed in the teen's name to help him or her begin to establish a credit history. Rent is split 50/50 with the mentor to allow the teen ownership in the apartment. The teen also works with the mentor to find an apartment in the greater Burlington vicinity. We require all teens to live on the bus line to help them establish independence from their roommate.

- The last and least restrictive program in our continuum is the **supervised apartment program**. This program replicates the closest thing to independence that the teen will see prior to discharge from our program. In this program, teens live alone or with an approved roommate. All teens are encouraged to work either part- or full-time. The program places strong emphasis on education. Teens are required to enroll in a diploma program, GED, or vocational program. After receiving a diploma or GED, teens can opt to attain a higher level of education. The stipend in this program is considerably smaller than in either the wraparound or mentor program. While enrolled in this program, teens are encouraged to monitor their own money. This task is accomplished with the support and guidance of their case manager. Teens are still required to be working on goals. The average length of stay in this program ranges between 3 and 6 months.

Staffing

The CBL program has the capacity to service up to 27 youth. We currently have a director, a coordinator, three case managers, and a recruiter/trainer. The recruiter/trainer works with a small number of youth.

The director oversees the larger issues facing the program, such as fiscal operations and securing funding, as well as overseeing the Transitional Independent Living program. The coordinator's responsibilities include oversight of the day-to-day operations and supervision of the case managers and the recruiter/trainer. The coordinator also works closely with other programs to secure referrals into the programs. The case managers provide support to the teens and to the mentors or foster parents. Case managers provide therapeutic services to the teen and his/her team. The recruiter/trainer recruits and screens all foster parents and mentors, and is responsible for providing monthly and state-mandated trainings.

Funding Sources

The primary funding source for the foster care program is the Department of Social and Rehabilitative Services (SRS). The other independent living programs receive funding from the Departments of Education, Mental Health, and Corrections. We also accept private funds. The funding options are separate as well as melded, depending on the financial arrangements of the teen.

Program Strengths and Needs

The main strength of our program is our ability to effectively provide required services as a team. We have the necessary flexibility in our planning process. Working as a team, however, can become a liability if funding resources are not adequate to support the team approach. We need more grant options and stepped-up insurance coverage.

Assessment of Client Strengths and Needs

We assess client strengths and needs through two potential avenues. The preferred route is for the teen to live for 1 to 3 months in our Phase

One program. While in this program, teens are required to meet specific assessment goals and, with program staff, identify areas in which they are weak. We look for a certain level of responsibility and motivation, as well as a commitment to the process. Assessments occur with the guidance of the program coordinator, residential manager, case manager, SRS worker, family, and any mental health clinicians who are involved with the teen. Teens are empowered through this process to develop a set of goals that will follow them as they transition through the different programs within the Spectrum family. Clients are encouraged to give feedback on their specific program and ways to improve it. Teens are very much part of the development process, and their feedback is very important to the growth of the CBL program.

Costs

The inclusive per diem for each of the living options varies from $46 to $117, depending on the specific program and staffing needs. This changes each year as our program is evaluated.

Who Signs the Lease and Why?

If there is a lease agreement involved, both the teen and the mentor sign. Through the teens' start-up monies, we provide them with the security deposit. The security deposit will travel with them after they leave the program if they meet their designated goals. Rents in our community are $550 and up. We encourage teens not to rent apartments for more than $650. This has proven difficult, since the program is housed in a college community.

Prior to the lease signing, the case manager has a discussion with the landlord explaining our program and the risks in renting to a teen. We find that most landlords are willing to rent to a teen/mentor after we assure them that these teens have been screened for program appropriateness. We have found that, if a teen moves into our supervised apartment program and lives with more than one roommate, there are problems, e.g., the other person not paying his or her portion of the rent, having guests over who use alcohol or other substances, and having a boyfriend or girlfriend over continuously. We have learned over the years to require a roommate to split the security deposit, as well as to get his or her name on the lease.

Client Comment

"I needed to fail with people there to help me...my family never gave me that chance...they were always busy criticizing my failure."

How Success is Measured

Success in our program is measured through goal completion and other designated measures that teens and their case managers have developed. We are currently developing a set of outcome measures that will be used within our programs.

Our Most Common Problems with Clients

1. Youth who have difficulty monitoring the appropriateness of people in their apartment.

2. Youth who have difficulty with their hygiene.

3. Youth who are unappreciative of the program, i.e., who "milk it" while in the program, but do not want to do the necessary work for discharge.

4. Youth who miss work, appointments, or meetings.

5. Clients with mental health disorders.

6. Damage caused to an apartment.

Things Staff Would Like to See Happen

■ Develop better funding mechanisms.

■ Remove state guidelines required by SRS. The staff feels this would allow them more flexibility in their approach.

■ Acquire ownership of apartments, so that teens would have greater access to affordable housing.

■ More awareness in society about adolescent independence and why it's necessary.

■ Higher pay for the work our teens do, so they can earn a higher monthly income.

■ Be able to provide driver's education for all teens, given our rural location.

■ Allow phone bill to be placed in a 16-year-old's name (with the appropriate blocks).

■ Be able to continue providing services to teens who exit the program due to age rather than readiness.

Most Common Staff-Related Problems

1. Lack of thorough communication about clients prior to weekend.

2. Logistical issues when clients move.

3. Keeping up with the ever-mounting paperwork required by a variety of sources.

4.Caseload overload.

5. Underpaid/overworked staff.

6. Too many meetings and not enough time for client contact.

Screening Mentors

Mentors are usually recruited into the CBL program through one of two methods — word-of-mouth or a want ad. After an initial letter of inquiry or phone call, the recruiter asks potential mentors to submit a resume and cover letter detailing the following:

1. What skills/experience can they bring to the relationship with a mentee?

2. What is their current life experience?

3. Who are they?

After the cover letter and resume are submitted, the prospective mentor sets up an initial meeting during which the recruiter details the position and timeline of the mentor hiring process. The recruiter assesses level of commitment and current life situation (e.g., is there a partner involved? are there any children from a previous relationship? is there a necessity to find a living situation?).

If the initial meeting finds both the recruiter and mentor in agreement, then a second interview is set up. It is important that the second meeting be at least a week after the initial meeting. We believe that the mentor needs time to "soul search" why s/he wants to live with a teen and begin to develop a list of questions and concerns about this type of living situation.

In the second meeting we focus on the person and his/her life experience, paying particular attention to his/her own adolescence. Questions we might ask include the following:

"What is the most traumatic experience you recall about being a teenager?"
"How did you deal with it?"

"What is the one type of teen that makes you the most nervous?"

Through these questions we try to get at potential problems that could arise between the mentor and mentee. We also take this time to answer any questions that might have arisen from the first meeting.

Finally, there is a third meeting. By this time, 2-4 weeks have elapsed. This is crucial, because it allows us to see the commitment that a potential mentor is willing to make. Individuals who are looking to do this because of the benefits, i.e., shared rent and utilities, often do not complete the process. In the third meeting the program is discussed in detail. Often a case manager and/or program coordinator is brought into this meeting. We discuss a variety of scenarios to assess responses, experiences, and potential problem areas, such as stealing, bringing inappropriate peers into the apartment, and/or general disrespect from the mentee towards the mentor or vice versa.

If all interviews have gone as hoped and the prospective mentor remains interested, then references are checked. We ask candidates to give us the name of at least one roommate who lived with them for a minimum of 6 months. If they can provide more than the one reference, that is encouraged.

The complete process can take from 1 to 2 months. Throughout, we get to know the interested candidate, and s/he is getting to know our program style and expectations. The initial meeting between mentor and mentee occurs outside the agency after initial introductions by the case manager. We encourage both parties to take as long as needed to determine if they could room together. The case manager has discussed with the mentee possible questions s/he should ask the mentor regarding concerns, likes, and dislikes. The same has occurred with the mentor. If both feel this is a match, then they move to the next phase of the process. If either feels that the two of them are not compatible, then the process begins anew. We try hard to ensure a successful match. That is why the process can take upwards of 2 months. We do not want potential mentors or mentees who are overly anxious to the point where they will sabotage their living situation. We have had a high success rate with this model. Most mentors live with two teens for a minimum of 6 months. The living situations can go longer if funding is available. It is not uncommon for the mentor and mentee to become lifelong friends after this shared living experience.

2
Youth Continuum Independent Living Services

New Haven, Connecticut

Denise Short and Meg Haffner

Brief History

Youth Continuum, Inc. is a private, non-profit, community-based, multi-service agency providing emergency shelter, group home living, transitional living, and prevention services to youth 3-23 years old throughout the State of Connecticut. Founded in 1968 as the nation's first Training and Research Institute-Residential Youth Center (TRI-RYC), Youth Continuum, Inc. has been licensed by the State of Connecticut Department of Children and Families since 1973.

Serving approximately 1,000 youth annually, Youth Continuum, Inc. (YCI) operates a number of diverse programs designed to meet the needs of children and youth. These programs include the following:

- Group Homes (Forbes House and UNO House)

- Emergency Shelter (Douglas House)

- Alternative Detention Program (JUST)

- Juvenile Supervision and Reporting Center (OASIS)

- Transitional Living Programs (CHAP, HUD, TLAP)

- Community Drop-In Youth Center and Outreach Services (HOSTS)

- Safe Home (Cleary House)

YCI provides a true "continuum" of care within the agency, allowing clients to transition smoothly from, for example, Forbes House to CHAP, or HUD to CHAP, or TLAP to HUD, under the guidance and cooperation of each component involved.

Mission

Believing that children are society's most valuable resource, Youth Continuum strives to meet the needs of at-risk youth and their families. We seek to protect and promote their well-being and preserve cultural heritage through the provision of emergency, residential, and community services for youth and their families.

Goals

1. To achieve satisfaction with our services among the youth and families with whom we interact.

2. To reunite youth with their families when it is in the youth's best interest.

3. To maintain a professional, compassionate, and diverse staff and ensure the highest quality care for youth.

4. To help youth integrate into the community and become functioning, independent adult members of the community.

This chapter focuses on the Community Housing Assistance Program (CHAP), but it also includes information on HOSTS and HUD, as the three work closely with each other, often serving the same client in different capacities.

Community Housing Assistance Program (CHAP)

Youth Continuum, Inc.'s Community Housing Assistance Program (CHAP) assists young adults as they make the transition from a supervised living arrangement to self-sufficiency. Homeless youth and youth from the child welfare system learn the skills necessary to live independently and to avoid long-term dependence on the social service system. Transitional living services are provided for 17 to 23 year olds who are able to live independently with minimal supervision. Case Managers work with the youth to create realistic work and educational goals. CHAP residents are enrolled in an educational or vocational program full-time and employed part-time. Youth are taught the skills needed to live independently, such as budgeting, how to find and keep a job, nutrition, home maintenance, and educational planning.

Youth who participate in CHAP are referred from the Department of Children and Families (DCF) or through the homeless youth outreach program at HOSTS (Helping Our Society To Survive). CHAP started in 1994 with one youth living in her own apartment and has grown to over 40 participants. The average length of stay is 18 months. Clients are able to remain in their apartments upon completion of the program. Leases are then in the clients' names, and the clients are responsible for paying the rent each month.

Helping Our Society To Survive (HOSTS)

Founded in 1978, HOSTS provides a safe and structured environment for at-risk and homeless youth to acquire the skills needed to become productive and contributing members of society. In 1995, HOSTS associated with Youth Continuum, Inc. to ensure its continued success, to expand its programming, and to focus on homeless, runaway, and at-risk youth.

Located in downtown New Haven, where vulnerable youth are most likely to congregate, HOSTS is a gateway to creating a better life. HOSTS allows youth to walk into a safe place without fear of being labeled or turned away. Staff at HOSTS provide a non-threatening, informal setting for youth, guided by the philosophy that every individual has the capacity for self-improvement and self-fulfillment.

At HOSTS, youth have access to a range of services. These include medical, dental, educational, psychological, recreational, therapeutic, and vocational services, as well as arts, substance abuse counseling, youth empowerment groups, and a Youth Advisory Board. Youth also participate in community events. HOSTS is open 6 days a week and typically serves 25 to 50 youth each day.

The Outreach Program focuses on outreaching to homeless youth in New Haven neighborhoods. Youth workers are actively involved in this effort. On-site case coordinators assist homeless youth in accessing services, arrange emergency shelter and transitional housing, and coordinate with other local agencies in providing services.

Assistance from Housing and Urban Development (HUD)

Once participants are deemed in need of housing, they are assigned to a Case Manager within YCI's CHAP (Community Housing Assistance Program). CHAP offers six Housing and Urban Development (HUD)-funded, scattered-site apartments for homeless youth 17-23 years of age. While youth are residing in these apartments, our Case Managers, the youth, and the HOSTS staff work on a discharge plan. The goal is to locate safe, permanent housing for homeless youth who have limited resources.

Staff Comment

"I think the program is a great resource for clients, whether they admit it or not. It is great to be able to receive assistance with education and housing as well as community life skills!"

Prior to selecting appropriate youth into a transitional apartment, a treatment team (consisting of the youth, the HOSTS Program Director, HOSTS Client Coordinators, and the CHAP Case Manager) conducts a comprehensive assessment. The assessment consists of determining if the youth is in need of various services, such as an educational placement, employment, child care, Department of Social Service funds, substance abuse treatment, psychiatric services, medical services, and housing. Of the 94 referrals made in 1999, 8 did not meet the definition of homeless. A total of 18 youth participated in our homeless program during the operating year, with an average length of stay of 4-6 months. Forty-six percent or 44 of the 94 referrals were placed on a waiting list due to lack of openings. Because of the high volume of appropriate referrals and the limited number of beds available (six), our treatment team meets once a week to review the current caseload and the waiting list. Many of the 44 who remained on the waiting list during the year temporarily lived with friends, at shelters, or with extended family members until an opening was available within our program.

YCI's objectives were to coordinate intake services and to provide transitional housing and comprehensive case management to New Haven area homeless youth, who reside in temporary HUD-funded housing. Within the first reporting year (September 1, 1997 to August 1, 1998), 22 youth successfully entered the HUD-funded program. Ninety-four youth were referred to the program, and 44 currently remain on a waiting list. Seventy-six referrals did not enter the program for the following reasons: there were no vacancies, they did not meet the minimum age requirement, they were not categorized as homeless as described by the HUD definition, or they refused services and returned home to live with family members. This reporting year (September 1, 1998 to August 1, 1999), 18 young adults (12 single youth and 6 young mothers with 7 children) were housed in our homeless program. Although we served 4 fewer youth than the previous reporting year, the 18 who participated in our program this reporting year remained in the program for an average of 6-8 months, or 1-3 months longer than last year. One third of our annual census were young mothers, typically with one child, and 5 out of the 7 children were under the age 1. One of the many challenges to providing permanent resident stability this year was locating affordable housing and child care for young mothers. YCI has responded to a federal RFP for a transitional living program providing additional beds for homeless youth with a longer length of stay.

Description of the Program

YCI Independent Living Program Objectives

YCI's objectives are to assist young people in making a successful transition to self-sufficiency and to prevent long-term dependence on the social services system. Interventions consist of guidance, support, and exercises designed to develop independent living skills and promote personal growth. To fulfill this purpose, case management is provided, rules are enforced, and individual goals and objectives are developed. Goals focus on educational, vocational, social, and interpersonal development.

Outline of Program Services

Housing. Apartments are selected based on their proximity to the educational facility of, and mode of transportation used by, each individual client; they are secured through the efforts of both YCI and the client. For mothers, two-bedroom apartments are ideal; for non-parenting clients, one-bedroom apartments are leased. Furnishings are supplied by donations and/or are purchased by the client (retail, tag sales, etc.). Leases are signed and security deposit paid by YCI/DCF. Upon successful completion of CHAP, clients may sign the lease (after applying to the landlord), keep the furniture, and claim the security deposit.

Financial Support. Rent is paid directly to the landlord by YCI. Clients receive a monthly stipend from DCF to expend on budget items. Bills and receipts are submitted to the Case Manager in order to monitor compliance with budgeting. The monthly stipend is detailed as follows:

Food	$159.00
Utilities	55.00
Telephone	30.00
Transportation	50.00
Clothing	53.50
Miscellaneous	60.00
TOTAL	**$407.50**

Utility and phone bills are put in the client's name as soon as possible (18 years old). For those whose rent does not include heat, energy assistance is available through the town/city and YCI. Quarterly DCF contracts include a budget, based on the client's income and designed to increase savings monthly to ensure financial independence upon completion of CHAP. Clients are required to work at least part-time. Clients under the age of 18 who are the custodial parent of a minor child or children enroll in Temporary Aid to Needy Families (TANF) through the Department of Social Services (DSS). TANF provides daycare for the youth's school attendance, as well as medical coverage and financial payments for the minor child(ren). DCF is responsible for any daycare expenses incurred by the youth for work-related purposes. Clients 18 years old or older who are the custodial parent of a minor child or children receive financial assistance from DCF. These payments include funds for the youth's living needs, financial payment for the minor child(ren) of $100 per month per child (this rate does not increase with additional births), and daycare for school/work. Medical coverage for the minor child(ren) continues to be provided by DSS. DCF also provides parenting clients with major equipment needs, such as crib and mattress, stroller, car seat, and diaper bag. Additional major equipment items, such as special medical equipment, playpen, and back-pack carrier, may be purchased for the committed adolescent parent if there is a demonstrated need. As clients progress in the program, they are expected to increase their income, thereby weaning themselves off of the monthly stipend. The stipend amount is expected to decrease quarterly.

Client Comment

"When I walked into your agency in the summer of 1995 you accepted me with open arms, and I thank you. When I had no where to go you guys gave me an apartment and helped me get back on my feet. You all have been by my side and supported me on all my positive journeys and aspirations. I consider you all to be good friends and hope that we can all keep in touch and never forget each other."

Life Skills Training. Clients are required, at the time of acceptance into CHAP, to have completed or to be enrolled in life skills classes. Clients take the Daniel Memorial Assessment every 6 months; Case Managers then concentrate on training in those areas where improvement is needed. Monthly CHAP groups are conducted to improve social skills and to continue to work on general life skills topics.

Emotional Support/Guidance. Clients are referred by their individual DCF Social Worker and maintain this relationship throughout their stay in CHAP. CHAP Case Managers are assigned approximately eight clients and are required to spend at least 5 hours on each client per week. Therapy is strongly suggested for each incoming client and, in some cases, is deemed a prerequisite for acceptance into CHAP. CHAP Case Managers are available by pager 24 hours a day, 7 days a week. Clients understand that they are able to contact *any* Case Manager at *any* time, especially in a crisis.

Case Management/Planning. Various community resources are utilized in order to wean clients off of the social services system and to have support in place upon discharge from the CHAP program. Job searching/training, educational training, social services, individual counseling, substance abuse counseling, legal needs, and parenting classes are just some of the services CHAP makes available to clients. These services are located in the general community so as to be accessible to clients at any time.

Average Daily Population

Currently, there are approximately 40 clients in CHAP; there is no limit to the number of clients accepted. An increase in referrals is seen typically in June (potential clients graduating from high school) and August (potential clients preparing to enter higher education in September). HUD is able to serve 6 clients at any given time.

Geographical Range — Areas Served

CHAP is a statewide program, serving the entire state of Connecticut. Cities and towns where CHAP apartments are or have been located include but are not limited to:

- Hartford
- New Britain
- New Haven
- Meriden
- West Hartford
- Wallingford
- West Haven
- Bethel
- Bristol
- Bridgeport
- Hamden
- Danbury

Clients have the opportunity to attend any school in Connecticut. If they choose to attend out-of-state schools, case management is provided on an as-needed basis, and housing is made available during summers and breaks.

Staffing

Position	Responsibilities
Chief Executive Officer	Supervises Director of Program Operations.
Director of Program Operations	Directly supervises CHAP Program Coordinator and HOSTS Program Director.

Program Coordinator

Trains and supervises Case Managers and Interns;

Oversees the development, implementation, and coordination of the clinical aspects of the program;

Oversees coordination of youth's progress through the program (pre-placement, intake, discharge, aftercare);

Oversees budget;

Case manages clients as assigned;

Conducts weekly Team Meetings;

Attends quarterly meetings with DCF Regional Coordinators;

Attends available conferences and trainings to enhance positive youth development;

On-call 24/7.

CHAP/HUD Case Managers (6)

Oversee the progress of a caseload of approximately eight clients;

Interview potential youth; assist in moving-in/out process;

Provide case management services to youth;

Provide transportation to youth as needed;

Communicate with youth's school, employer, and others to ensure youth's progress;

Facilitate monthly independent life skills groups;

Provide referral, advocacy, crisis intervention, and counseling services to youth;

Connect clients with community resources;

Provide supervision (at least 5 hours per week per client) to ensure safety and stability, including unannounced visits and 24/7 on-call coverage;

Collaborate with DCF Social Workers and youth on development

| CHAP/HUD Case Managers (cont.) | of quarterly contracts;
Complete Daniel Memorial Life Skills Assessments with clients on a regular basis;
Provide in-service training to all YCI staff on independent living issues;
Establish a network of landlords throughout the state;
Participate in ongoing agency training and Team Meetings;
Responsible for documentation (client progress reports submitted to DCF on a monthly basis). |
| **Interns** | Assist Case Managers with monitoring client progress and above responsibilities. |

Funding Sources

- Connecticut Department of Children and Families (CHAP)

CHAP Case Managers are paid a per diem rate of $53.98/client (as of January 2000) on a billable basis. Other per diem rates are as follows: the transitional living apartment program (TLAP) $50/client; the group homes $150/client; the shelter $160/client; and the safe home $170/client. This income alone covers all line items in CHAP's budget.

- Housing and Urban Development federal grant (HUD)

- City funding (HOSTS)

   For example, Title IV-E independent living funds for training.

- Private donations

Assessment of Client Strengths and Needs

Program rules dictate expected client conduct and responsibilities. Referrals completed by DCF and prospective clients include direct questions concerning strengths and needs. After clients are established in the program, their strengths and needs are determined more accurately through the daily and weekly contact of Case Managers. Assessment is also based on feedback from therapists, Social Workers, and family;

Daniel Memorial Independent Living Assessment scores; case plan reviews; educational grades (especially semester to semester); length of employment (or appropriateness in changing jobs); goal accomplishment; adherence to budgeting (submission of bills/receipts, bank statements); and monthly Case Manager reports. In general, continued compliance or noncompliance with program expectations demonstrates individual strengths and needs.

Life Skills Training Strategies

> **Staff Comment**
>
> "I find that I need to be creative with the client's treatment plan, as each individual has different needs. I am always interested in outside resources and groups to get the clients involved socially."

Referring clients are required to have completed (and they need to show proof of completion) or be enrolled in a life skills program. Clients are expected to complete the Daniel Memorial Independent Living Assessment every 6 months to determine progress of life skills knowledge. Monthly CHAP Group Meetings are held, focusing on areas which clients and Case Managers have seen as common needs within the population and/or as timely topics. Case Managers also deal with more individualized needs of their particular caseload on a daily basis, working with clients on areas that need improvement.

Client Involvement in Program Development

Potential clients (i.e., those in the group homes or who associate with a current client) are encouraged to consult their Social Worker about CHAP information. They are invited to visit the CHAP offices to discuss program requirements. If they are deemed eligible, their Social Worker sends a referral to their Supervisor and to the Regional Independent Living Coordinator. The referral, along with a recommendation, is sent to YCI. A pre-placement meeting is scheduled with the potential client, his/her Social Worker, and his/her Case Manager(s) to determine an appropriate timeline of acceptance to CHAP. The timeline depends on such factors as whether s/he has met enough goals, has proper ID to cash checks, is attending school/work/therapy consistently, and has a savings account.

During the pre-placement meeting, clients are given the responsibility to gather necessary paperwork (e.g., birth certificate and Social Security card). Clients are encouraged to look for appropriate housing on their own, in addition to the efforts of the Case Managers. Clients are responsible for communicating their needs regarding such things as transportation for moving and furniture. Contact continues between the Social Worker, the Case Manager, and the client to determine various housing-related needs. A date is set for move-in, based on completion of the CHAP contract, move-in shopping for basic supplies, etc. Once established in CHAP, clients are required to attend and participate in monthly CHAP Group Meetings. They are encouraged to attend regional and statewide Youth Advisory Boards, as well as to represent YCI/DCF at collaboratives throughout the country. It is through these channels that many new policies have been created (e.g., continuance in CHAP until age 23 and minor child expenses of $100/month).

Open communication is continued between YCI, DCF, and the client throughout the client's stay in CHAP. Clients work with a mentor on talking with the landlord/superintendent to establish a working relationship and possible future housing.

Types of Housing Options Utilized by the Program

Descriptions of Current CHAP Housing Options

Most of our clients live in individual scattered-site apartments. At present, two of our clients are roommates. A host home in Danbury has been utilized in the past. Clients going away to school or who are with us during summers and breaks from school live primarily in campus housing (dormitories). Upon nearing completion of CHAP, clients are encouraged to find (with case management assistance) affordable housing if the apartment they are currently in is above their means. "Affordable" may mean finding a roommate and/or living in a smaller apartment than made available in CHAP.

Cost of Various Housing Options

Regional Rent Allotments

(Rent rates change with cost-of-living increases; rents are paid by YCI from the per diem.)

Region I
(Southwest CT:
Bridgeport/Stamford)
$619-862

Region II
(South Central CT:
New Haven/Middletown/
Meriden) $419-655

Region III
(Eastern CT:
Norwich/Willimantic)
$445-583

Region IV
(North Central CT:
Hartford/New Britain)
$504-609

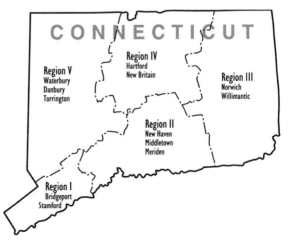

Region V
(Northwest CT: Waterbury/Danbury/ Torrington) $526-673

Problems Specific to Each Option

- **Scattered-site apartments:** Loneliness of client;
  Client's unfamiliarity with area;
  Music/TV/general noise too loud;
  Landlords treating clients like criminals;
  Noncompliance with lease/program
    rules;
  Unwanted or too many visitors;
  Unwanted pets;
  Inability of client to afford apartment
    upon completion of program;
  Family/friends attempting to live with
    client;
  Runaways finding refuge in apartment;
  Minors visiting in the apartment;
  Damage;
  Restoring cleanliness of apartment when
    problematic client leaves;
  Untrusting/suspicious neighbors;
  Getting a lease in client's name (some
    landlords will not do it);
  Hygiene/housekeeping issues.

- **Roommates:** Splitting bills;
  Sharing housekeeping responsibilities;
  Privacy.

- **Dormitories:** Need for housing/furniture during
    breaks/summers.

Liability/Risk Management Issues

Clients who are disruptive, destructive, or dangerous can be removed immediately. Landlords and superintendents are given pager numbers for 24-hour access to Case Managers. Periodic unannounced visits are conducted; they are increased and conducted at odd hours if deemed necessary for a particular client. Clients are made aware of agency policies regarding removal from the apartment. They are informed that YCI is the official tenant and has the right to remove them at any time, if circumstances warrant that.

Clients are expected to pay for damages as soon as possible from their savings. If unable to do so, clients are required to reimburse YCI or to set up a payment plan with their landlord. Damages from an "AWOL" client are paid for by YCI; the client's Social Worker is informed of the expense and, when able, may make arrangements with the client to reimburse YCI. YCI carries insurance for fire and relocation, among other things, but not for personal belongings.

Who Signs the Lease and Why?

Youth Continuum's Chief Executive Officer signs the lease. An addendum may be added, stating the current client's name (and children's names, if applicable) and YCI's right to replace one client with another (with appropriate notification to the landlord). This gives YCI more control over the apartment and avoids having to go through the legal eviction process when a client needs to be removed — an important selling point to landlords who would not normally rent to youth because of the potential negative issues.

Legally, clients cannot sign a lease if they are under 18 years old. Having YCI's Chief Executive Officer sign the leases therefore enables us to accept clients under the age of 18 and to find housing for them.

> **Staff Comment**
>
> *"I really like the one-on-one relationship that I can give my clients. I feel that I have a meaningful share in supporting them in their decision making."*

Once clients have proved that they are responsible tenants and can afford the rent, they may apply to the landlord through the regular process and possibly assume the lease from YCI. Or, if they need to move to a more affordable apartment, they can use the landlord as a reference.

What Seems to be Working in the YCI CHAP Program

We are a statewide program, which allows clients a choice to either live within their community or reside outside of their community to attend school. Our program is tailored to fit individual needs; apartment placement is determined by where the client will attend school. Employment and support systems are also included in case plans. CHAP Case Management services are available 24 hours a day and 7 days a week to offer support with education, employment, budgeting, community resources, apartment safety, medical care, etc. State Legislator and Commissioner of the Department of Children and Families offers support. The Department of Children and Families Social Worker, the Youth Continuum Case Manager, and the CHAP client immediately form a partnership.

Two Examples of YCI, Inc. Successes

Troy came into our program after being removed from his previous program. He had been labeled as someone who will "never succeed in life." However, our staff noticed Troy's determination to prove this not to be the case. His goal was to enroll and attend New York University. But with help and encouragement from our staff, Troy instead made the decision to attend a New Haven community college first. He realized that he needed to be better prepared academically for NYU and chose to work on improving his GPA while attending the community college. Troy worked hard to accomplish this and after 1 year was accepted at NYU. He then faced another obstacle: all services that Youth Continuum, Inc. and the Department of Children and Families offered, including his college tuition, would cease when he turned 21. Troy was still determined to graduate from NYU and was encouraged by YCI staff to advocate for himself by writing letters to the Commissioner and all other interested parties concerning this matter. Subsequently, because of Troy's determination to succeed, a bill was passed by the Commissioner to extend services from age 21 to age 23 for Connecticut CHAP clients who maintain a B average. Troy graduated from New York University with a BA in Fine Arts in May 2000 and now resides in New York City.

Crystal entered Youth Continuum Douglas House (shelter) at the age of 14 and was transferred to YCI Forbes House (group home) at age 15. She later entered the YCI CHAP program. With the support of YCI staff and the DCF Social Worker, and through Crystal's own determination, she was accepted at Yale University, where she is now in her second year. Although Crystal lives on campus, YCI provides her with housing during holidays and school breaks through the CHAP program. Crystal is presently an advocate for our CHAP program, speaking at fund-raisers and regional and national independent living conferences about her life and the benefits of the YCI CHAP program.

How Success is Measured

- Increased use of aftercare

- Positive feedback from DCF Social Workers and Supervisors

- Continued communication from graduated clients

- Independence from social services

- Healthy decision making

- Educational and financial goals met

- Savings account/checking account balanced

- Safety of clients
- Safe, clean living environments

- Careers

- Client income vs. outgo

- Driver's license

- Financial success

- Meeting established goals

- Creating new goals

- Signing own lease

- Positive completion/graduation from CHAP

- Maintaining good physical health

- Communicating effectively within the community

- Referral base

- Waiting list

- Continue to receive referrals

- Program expansion, as indicated by:
    - hiring more Case Managers
    - apartments becoming more widespread
    - new landlords participating

- Seeing positive changes made in DCF policy and legislation

- Client progress in each of the following IL areas:
    - money management and consumer awareness
    - food management and housekeeping
    - health and personal appearance/hygiene
    - education/training
    - employment
    - transportation
    - community resources
    - emergency and personal safety skills
    - interpersonal skills
    - legal skills or issues/needs
    - parenting issues
    - issues related to child if youth is parenting
    - housing

Our Top Ten Most Common Problems with Clients

1. Noise

2. Client's whereabouts unknown

3. Unwelcome pets

4. Visitors

5. Drug/alcohol issues

6. Pregnancy

7. Daycare payment (DCF)

8. School payment (DCF)

9. Clients' budgeting

10. Savings

The following are also common problems: mental health issues, loneliness, hygiene, apartment cleanliness, lack of success among clients coming from group homes, clients leaving prematurely and without a plan, and "entitled" clients.

Things Staff Would Like to See Happen

- Computers/Internet access

- Legislative representative/lobbyist
  HUD would benefit from a national spokesperson who could speak out against homelessness and educate America on behalf of homeless youth across the country.

- Increased funding/resources
  Recently YCI was awarded additional federal HUD funding to start up a transitional living apartment program (TLAP) for homeless youth. With this program funding, we will have the capability and an opportunity to provide longer term temporary housing and to service more of the homeless New Haven population. However, once a youth has successfully completed the program and taken advantage of the services offered, s/he con-

tinues to face the challenge of securing affordable housing. Given this, we recommend that there be an "automatic" linkage and/or availability of existing financial subsidies or programs (such as Section 8 or housing certificates) for homeless youth who complete our program, in order to keep them in permanent housing.

- Training

   Specifically, staff would like training on tracking discharged youth and measuring their level of success. Staff would also like further technical assistance or direct training on the most efficient way of maintaining data electronically.

- Continued networking with other similarly funded programs throughout the country via national conferences, workshops, and trainings

- Better communication among the staff throughout the week

- Working more effectively as a team

- Stopping or at least slowing the continuous increase of required paperwork

- Greater community involvement (e.g., area businesses contributing time and money to the program)

- Improved public relations

- Exposing clients to more experiences

- Continuum of clients from Group Homes to CHAP

- Reentry into CHAP if a discharged client realizes a need for the program after leaving prematurely

- A national or regional youth conference or forum to provide current and former HUD program participants an opportunity to share their experiences and discuss supportive services, creative living arrangements, etc.

Most Common Staff-Related Problems

1. Difficulties related to working as a team

2. High caseloads

3. Paperwork

4. Lack of effective communication with providers and within team

Termination and Giving Kids Second Chances

Youth who consistently break program rules are placed on Service Agreements. The purpose of these agreements is to spell out in clear, understandable terms the responsibilities that each party (client, YCI Case Manager, DCF Social Worker) has in creating the conditions that must exist to achieve the goal of continuation in YCI CHAP. For example, clients who consistently violate the visitors rule are instructed that they are not allowed to have visitors at all for a specified period of time; or clients who do not attend school on a regular basis may be asked to call into Case Managers daily and/or have school personnel sign a daily attendance sheet; substance abuse would require a drug evaluation and necessary counseling. It all depends on the individual and the issue. The agreement is reviewed after the allotted time. (Some agreements are ongoing.) If the client adheres to the contract, s/he may continue in CHAP.

If the client does not adhere to the contract, discharge plans will be discussed. An extension may be granted, depending on the client's progress regarding the issue. If a housing resource is available (i.e., a relative who is supportive of the client and of the CHAP philosophy and requirements), plans can be made for the client to live there for a determined period of time, to consider whether or not s/he wants to stay in CHAP. This often brings in an element of "life without CHAP and DCF," helping the client to appreciate the benefits of adhering to the rules. In the event of serious, continuous rule violation, YCI, DCF, and the client will meet to determine when the client will leave the program and where s/he will go.

Discharge from DCF means automatic discharge from YCI CHAP, with no chance of readmittance. Working with DCF, a plan is made to connect the client with the necessary community resources (e.g., relatives, Section 8, supervised living, HUD). Opportunity is given to bring the apartment lease to an appropriate close (unless YCI retains the lease for another client).

In cases where it is determined that the client can remain with DCF but is not appropriate for CHAP (e.g., serious mental health needs, serious substance abuse issues), resources are put into place to benefit the client's needs (e.g., supervised living, hospitalization). Readmittance into CHAP is possible and will be determined through continued contact between the client, DCF, and YCI.

3
Green Chimneys Life Skills Program

New York, New York

Gerald P. Mallon

Brief History

Green Chimneys Independent Living Program was established in 1986 to help meet the critical yet overlooked needs of older youth preparing to transition from foster care to independence. In 1990, our program shifted its focus to provide life skills services specifically for gay, lesbian, bisexual, transgendered, and questioning (GLBTQ) young people who we felt were at greatest risk.

After finding that a large group of former foster care youth were homeless and without adequate self-sufficiency skills, legal advocates for youth in foster care filed a class action lawsuit against the City and State of New York (*Palmer v. Koch*, 1980). The action sought to permit youth in foster care to remain until their 21st birthday, rather than discharging them to self at age 18. In response, the New York City child welfare administration agreed to a proposal made by our agency staff to allow us to try placing youth in independent living residences. Several years later, the administration agreed to place age-appropriate youth in scattered-site apartments in the borough of Manhattan. In 1999, we were awarded a Federal Runaway and Homeless Youth (RHY) Grant to develop and operate Transitional Living Programs (TLP) for GLBTQ runaway and homeless youth. All three Green Chimneys programs — the Gramercy Residence, the Supervised Independent Living Program (SILP), and the Transitional Living Program (TLP) — provide an array of services to youth from day one when they enter the program. These services, including financial assistance, intensive life skills development, case-management and support services, intensify several months before youth are discharged from the system.

Client Comment

"I think the one thing I wished I learned more about was the importance of saving money. I know that it was always something that the staff were telling me I should do, but I just had no idea how much it cost to live on your own. When you live in a group home you don't really have to worry about paying for anything, but boy, when you're on your own, you have to pay for everything!"

Over the years, this private/public collaboration has proven to be a valuable addition to the continuum of care for high-risk youth in New York City. As of 2000, Green Chimneys has served over 400 youth, many of whom have gone on to become productive, self-sufficient, responsible community members. Some of our former clients continue to work with the program in various training, mentoring, and advocacy roles. One former program participant said this about his experience at Green Chimneys: "If it wasn't for Green Chimneys, I think I would be dead by now. I was so messed up as a teenager, and even though I wasn't easy, the staff always stuck with me. I owe them a lot."

Green Chimney's life skills programs serve youth ages 16-21 years who have run away from home, or are in custody of New York City's foster care system, or are transitioning from juvenile corrections systems. The programs also serve youth from other New York localities outside the city and from three neighboring states — New Jersey, Connecticut, and

Pennsylvania. Non-systems youth, i.e., young adults ages 18-22 years who are not in the care of any system, are served by the agency's Transitional Living Program (TLP). These young people are referred from the adult homeless shelter system or from street outreach programs serving GLBTQ runaway and homeless youth.

Although some TLP clients were formerly in custody, very few were previously in an independent living program. The TLP is funded with Federal Runaway and Homeless Youth Act funds, HUD funds, foundation grants, and donations. The staff from the Life Skills Program and TLP interact frequently and act as resources to each other.

Description of the Program

The Green Chimneys Life Skills Program for GLBTQ youth utilizes the group residence and scattered-site apartment models. The Life Skills Program is not a separate entity but a significant component representing an integrated and interdisciplinary team approach. Putting it simply, the Life Skills Program is a component of the overall planning for all age-appropriate (16-21 years) residents.

Client Comment

"Some days are very hard. I guess no one ever said it would be easy, but I just had no idea how hard it would be. Rent is a big drag, it cost so much money to live in a decent place in New York City, and I am not talking about Manhattan, honey, I live in Queens – an outer borough. Never thought I'd move out there, but it's affordable, clean, and safe. All in all, hard as it is, I am proud of myself. I have done a lot more than most guys my age."

Green Chimneys Life Skills Objectives

Specific service objectives for this program include the following:

1. To provide stable and safe living accommodations for GLBTQ youth in need.

2. To provide intensive life-skills counseling to youth, individually and in groups, utilizing our own nationally recognized Green Chimneys curriculum, *Life Skills for Living in the Real World*.

3. To conduct individualized life skills assessment, utilizing our own Green Chimneys Life Skills Assessment instrument to assist the youth in the development of realistic life skills plans.

4. To assist youth in developing interpersonal skills by providing weekly group sessions, individual counseling, and a therapeutic environment with

an MSW-level social worker, as prescribed by our Green Chimneys Individualized Treatment Plans.

5. To conduct an individual educational assessment for all program youth and to develop a plan for educational advancement.

6. To assist youth in obtaining their high school diploma or GED at the agency and Board of Education-sponsored Audre Lorde High School or other community-based educational programs.

7. To conduct an individual substance abuse assessment for all program youth and to develop a plan for prevention, education, and treatment if indicated.

8. To conduct a complete medical screening and to provide access to health care services for all program youth with our health care partners at community-based adolescent clinics.

9. To assist youth in obtaining and maintaining employment in the community.

Client Comment

"I really wish I had listened more about going to school. I really struggled through high school and I hated it. But now I realize that I need much more than high school – I mean, people with a college degree are fighting for the same jobs that I am – in some cases, I don't have a chance. Because I hated high school so much, I could never see beyond just getting out. Now I know differently."

Outline of Program Services

Housing. Youth are provided with housing in either the Gramercy Life Skills Residence or one of the SILP or TLP apartments. They are assisted with obtaining housing in the community when they are discharged from the program.

■ Gramercy Life Skills Residence: provides residential life skills services for foster care youth (25 young males and transgendered youth, 16-20 years). The program specializes in providing programs and a safe environment for gay, bisexual, questioning, and transgendered young people.

■ Supervised Independent Living Program (SILP): provides residential services for foster care youth (14 young men in seven apartments, and 4 young women in two apartments). All residents are 18-20 years. Admission to this program is contingent upon high school graduation and an ability to handle a high degree of independence. The NYC-based SILP programs specialize in providing safe environments for gay, lesbian, bisexual, and transgendered young people.

■ Transitional Living Program (TLP): provides residential services (10 runaway and homeless young men and women in three scattered-site apartments). All residents are 18-20 years. Admission to this program is contingent upon meeting intake criteria for runaway or homeless youth. A central feature of this program is the development of life skills and the maintenance of an employment situation to achieve self-sufficiency within 18 months. The NYC-based TLPs specialize in providing safe environments for gay, lesbian, bisexual, and transgendered young people.

Life Skills Services. The Green Chimneys Life Skills Program consists of several components, which are described below:

■ Education: Every resident of our programs is required to attend and complete his or her high school education, working towards a regular high school diploma, a GED, or an IEP Diploma, as prescribed by the local Board of Education in cooperation with our agency treatment teams. In 1997, the agency, in collaboration with the New York City Board of Education, opened an Alternative High School for youth called the Audre Lorde High School. The Audre Lorde School is sited at a Green Chimneys facility and is a collaboration between Green Chimneys and the New York City Board of Education. Although the school is primarily geared toward Green Chimneys youth, any young person is eligible for admission. Youth who graduate are assisted in attending college.

■ Vocational Experience and Training: Every resident in any of the Life Skills programs is strongly encouraged to be employed during the summer months and in some cases on a full-time basis throughout the year, unless recommended otherwise by the team. During the school year, those students who are passing all of their subjects and have good attendance are permitted by the treatment team to engage in appropriate part-time employment. Job seeking and job maintenance skills development is

Client Comment

"It's the one place where I can come that everyone will always be happy to see me. I still come to see my social worker and the director — they were both very important people to me. I want them to see how good I'm doing. I visit because people here really cared for me. Even when I was in my own little fantasy world, they cared for me. I come back to see them. I come back when I need help. They even let me stay here for two weeks once when I lost my apartment and had no place to go, I mean most agencies would not do that for you. They really care for you, even after you're gone. Whenever I walk in that door, I am always welcomed — that's important — that you're always welcomed."

taught in the program by staff. Collaborators in the community conduct vocational testing and training, which are also important components of the life skills program.

■   Counseling and Support Services: Program caseworkers and primary counselors provide these services in weekly individual sessions. Sessions focus on goals set by the team and provide a forum for the resident and his or her counselor to discuss any issue pertaining to the program at Green Chimneys. Group sessions are also utilized as counseling interventions. There are ten different groups scheduled each week, dealing with issues such as depression, substance abuse, separation issues, sexuality, sexual abuse, and prostitution. All residents are required to participate in at least two groups (of their choice) per week.

Life Skills Activities, which are part of the overall program, can be described best in terms of the following components:

■ The Life Skills Coordinator (LSC) conducts the Initial Life Skills Assessment during the resident's first week of orientation into the program. The Initial Life Skills Assessment Scale enables the assessor to examine the resident in 15 areas and to determine areas of strength or need, based on a five-point GLAS (Green Chimneys Longitudinal Assessment Scale). The LSC develops priorities in areas of need, which can be translated into team goals, and gives credit in areas where the resident already has skills. The LSC then gives a complete report of this assessment at the Initial Clinical Case Conference, which occurs 1 month after admission. The Initial Life Skills Assessment is updated every 6 months at the semiannual Clinical Case Conference by the LSC, who documents progress in previously designated areas of need and determines areas that need continuing focus.

■ Life Skills Seminars are held on a weekly basis at Gramercy and in the SILP/TLP Resource Center. They are required for all age-appropriate residents. This forum is used to announce community activities and concerns, but guest speakers are also invited to share their insights and lives with residents. The areas discussed follow the 15 Life Skills units but also address a wide variety of other issues for all participants. Once a month sessions focus on human sexuality education.

■ The Life Skills Course is held weekly for all residents. This course uses our own curriculum, *Life Skills for Living in the Real World*, by Gerald P. Mallon, DSW, which is a comprehensive 15-unit curriculum guide based on the Initial Life Skills Assessment. The participants of this course are specifically taught essential skills necessary for living independently. Sessions consist of both experiential and lecture format. Sections are taught at the Gramercy Residence and in the SILP/TLP Resource Center or in the youth's apartment.

■ Life Skills Seminar Weekends are held several times throughout the year at the Green Chimneys Hillside Outdoor Educational Center in Brewster, New York. Groups of eight residents and three staff go to the country for a weekend. Each group selects a theme, develops a menu, shops for the food, prepares the food, and works together as a small community. Small group dynamics, based on the theme of the weekend, as well as recreational opportunities, such as hiking, swimming, horseback riding, high ropes courses, and basketball, make this weekend an experience which residents and staff enjoy.

Client Comment

"Boy, when they used to bug me about getting up in the morning and get me going to school, I had no idea how important that would be for my future. By the time I left I had a high school diploma and two years of college. Even that wasn't enough, but I know dudes out there with nothing! I finished my college degree last year. I am very happy that I had the head start that I had."

■ Life Skills Cultural Events: On a semiannual basis, residents participate in special cultural events, which are designed to expose them to happenings in the New York area. In the past, residents have dined in an "elegant" restaurant, attended theater productions and movies, and visited local museums. Progress notes document individual participation, and these are filed in the resident's individual case record.

■ Savings/Stipends: Every resident is directly given a monthly Life Skills stipend by check ($20-$40, depending on age) and is urged to save it. Residents are also encouraged to have a bank account. The Life Skills Coordinator assists youngsters in opening a savings account at local banks. Residents hold their own bank books and are completely responsible for depositing and withdrawing funds.

■ Aftercare Services: These services are provided by our caseworkers. Ninety days before discharge, residents are notified by the program director in writing, on agency letterhead, and are instructed to work with their caseworker and the treatment team to secure appropriate and affordable housing.   Caseworkers and primary counselors address issues regarding separation.   Any resident who is discharged before his or her 21st birthday is discharged on a trial basis and is followed up for a mandated 6-month period.   During this period, monthly face-to-face contacts are made, with at least one visit in the resident's home.   The agency is responsible for providing information and referral services and supervision after the 6-month final discharge period.   Residents who are discharged on their 21st birthday are informally followed up by staff.   There are no requirements for aftercare for this group, but the agency is committed to following up all former program participants.   Former residents are always welcome to visit and have frequently asked for additional assistance when needed.   Even though we are not mandated to perform this service and are not reimbursed for it, Green Chimneys is strongly committed to assisting our young people, both those in our care and those who have passed through our programs.

> **Client Comment**
>
> "Man, I had no idea! When I tried to get a loan they asked about credit, did I have a credit history. I mean, I remember hearing about this, but I never really paid much attention to it. Now I wished that I had."

Average Daily Population

Our average daily population is currently around 53 youth.   Between 1986 and 1999, we averaged 45 youth a day.

Geographical Range — Areas Served

Green Chimneys youth are primarily from New York City, but are also from the outlying metropolitan area within a 50-mile radius, as well as from three neighboring states: New Jersey, Connecticut, and Pennsylvania. Youth in the TLP program come from many different areas throughout the United States.

Staffing

Life Skills Program staff positions and job responsibilities are listed below:

■ Associate Executive Director for New York City Programs acts as the director of this program for the entire agency.   Responsibilities are to read, interpret, and disseminate to involved staff all correspondence from the local, state, and federal authorities with regard to Independent Living.   In addition, the director submits the quarterly reports, monitors compliance, and insures the effective operation of the program throughout the agency.

This is a full-time position, supervised by the Executive Director and based at the New York City agency headquarters located in Harlem.

■ Director of the Gramercy Residence acts as the administrator of the Gramercy Life Skills Residence. Responsibilities include supervision of social work, life skills, child care, and education staff. In addition, the director provides day-to-day supervision of the Gramercy program.

■ Coordinators of the SILP act as administrators for the scattered-site apartment program for foster care youth. Responsibilities include supervision of social work, life skills, counselor, and education staff. In addition, coordinators provide day-to-day supervision of the SILP.

■ Coordinator of the TLP acts as the administrator of the scattered-site apartment program for runaway and homeless youth. Responsibilities include supervision of social work, life skills, counselor, and education staff. In addition, the coordinator provides day-to-day supervision of the TLP.

■ The Life Skills Coordinators (one for Gramercy Residence and one for the SILP/TLPs) are responsible for seeing that each resident has a vocational test and that the recommendations based on that test are followed up. LSCs complete the Initial Life Skills Assessment during the orientation period and complete a 6-month update there-

Client Comment

"The people in this program saved my life. I know that sounds very dramatic, and sometimes I am accused of being dramatic, but I really believe it! When I lived at Green Chimneys I was a messed up person. They stuck with me and even now, 13 years after I was discharged, whenever I call, they are always genuinely happy to hear from me. They always make me feel so good and some days I need to feel good about myself. They have done so much for me, I will always be grateful to the staff at Green Chimneys."

after, focusing on needs and assisting the treatment team in formulating appropriate Life Skills goals in these identified areas. LSCs teach job seeking skills to residents who are seeking employment; teach job maintenance skills to those who are employed; and arrange for vocational training for those who need to develop skills. In addition, LSCs follow up on a monthly basis on those who are employed, making sure that they are doing well. LSCs schedule all Life Skills Seminars; teach the Life Skills Course; and coordinate all of the Life Skills Weekend Seminars at Hillside. LSCs report to the Associate Executive Director and are based in New York City at the Gramercy Residence and the SILP/TLP Resource Center.

■ The Education Coordinator (one based in New York City) completes an Initial Education Assessment on each resident during orientation, enrolls residents in appropriate educational placements, follows up on these students on a weekly basis, and supervises the tutors. In addition, the Education Coordinator conducts a weekly educational group, which involves group discussions and visits to various cultural sites in the New York City area. This worker also assists in teaching the Life Skills Course and participates in planning all of the Life Skills weekly and weekend seminars. The Education Coordinator reports to the Associate Executive Director.

Client Comment

"Everybody here was trying to help me; sometimes I just didn't let them help me. I was living in my own fantasy world. I didn't get it. But I sure got it when I left, I can tell you that! It ain't no fantasy world out there in the real world – it's hard. It's a lot of work, but it feels good knowing I'm taking care of me. It's also good to know that when I look around my apartment, that everything that's there is mine!"

■ The Substance Abuse Coordinator (one based in New York City) completes an Initial Substance Abuse Assessment on each resident during orientation, enrolls residents in appropriate treatment programs (if necessary), follows up on these youth on a weekly basis, and supervises the substance abuse training for all staff. In addition, the coordinator conducts a weekly prevention group, which involves group discussions and training sessions. The coordinator also assists in teaching the Life Skills Course and participates in planning all of the Life Skills weekly and weekend seminars. The coordinator reports to the Associate Executive Director.

■ Social workers (two MSW-level persons) facilitate groups, conduct individual sessions, document treatment plans for the case record, and provide aftercare for the youth.

■ Life Skills Secretary does typing and filing and maintains all Life Skills information for the case record.

Funding Sources

The majority of Green Chimneys funding (59%) comes from per diem contracts with local children's services, paid at a state aid rate. The agency also receives special independent living allotments of $2,700 per youth, per year, for all youth over 14 years.

Funds are also received from the following sources:

■ Private donations,

- Federal Runaway and Homeless Youth grants,

- Agency fund-raising efforts, and

- Client purchase of service fees.

Assessment of Client Strengths and Needs

This is an ongoing process that involves feedback from the youth, referring agency caseworker, previous caregivers, and Life Skills Coordinators. The team meets weekly to review each case, with the youth's input. Every 6 months a complete review (called a Service Plan Review) is conducted with all disciplines and the youth to evaluate progress.

Life Skills Training Strategies

We teach life skills in several ways in our program. It all begins with an individual initial assessment, which then creates goals to be addressed either individually or in small groups with the youth. This initial assessment is updated every 6 months, with new goals developed to focus on areas of need and credit given for those areas where there are strengths. The formal sessions, which are held in a group instruction style, are supplemented with experiential training sessions, cultural seminars, and weekend retreats. One-on-one relationship building and development of the youth's potential are at the core of all Green Chimneys life skills programs.

Client Involvement in Program Development

From day one, youth are involved along with staff in their team's decisions. Meetings about the youth are held only when the youth are present, and youth are provided with documentation to back up the decisions made at these meetings.

Types of Housing Options Utilized by Green Chimneys

Twenty-eight of our youth live in individual scattered-site apartments. Eighteen foster care youth live in SILP apartments; ten runaway and homeless youth live in TLP apartments. We also have a large four-story group residence that is staffed 24 hours a day and houses 25 youth.

Descriptions of Current Green Chimneys Housing Options

- Individual scattered-site apartments — 12 two- or three-bedroom, fully furnished apartments in the community, with staff on call.

- Group residence — a large townhouse with 15 double and/or private bedrooms, on-site school, full array of services, and 24-hour staff.

Cost of Various Housing Options

We receive a basic rate of $89 per day per client in the SILP program, $196 per day in the Gramercy Program, and a Federal block grant of $184,000 per year provides funding for the TLP program. We receive additional rates for Medicaid, Substance Abuse, and Independent Living program expenses. The program requires additional funds for youth with special needs who need daily staff contact.

Problems Specific to Each Option

- **Scattered-site apartments:** Theft of food and clothing and others' belongings;
  Arguments about visitors, music, use of phones, cooking;
  Blaming of roommate for problems, damages, and messes;
  Noisy clients;
  Conflict with friends or family members;
  Allowing visitors to live in the apartments;
  Poor hygiene skills;
  Occasional damages;
  Moving evicted clients;
  Client loneliness.

- **Group residence:** Problems due to mix of clients;
  Staff burnout;
  Arguments over food, theft, bathroom cleanliness, telephone and TV use;
  Blaming other residents for problems;
  Breaking rules when day staff is gone;
  Calls from neighbors about group gatherings or noise.

Who Signs the Lease and Why?

The lease is signed in the agency's name. We do this first and foremost because landlords would not rent to residents who are young and who have potentially unstable employment. Apartments in New York City are very expensive; our cheapest two-bedroom apartment is $900 per month.

We also do this to maintain control of the apartment. If a youth doesn't work out in a particular apartment, we can then replace or terminate him or her, because the apartment belongs to the agency, not to the individual.

We initially hoped that if a youth had a job and had proven to be a responsible tenant, then we would allow him/her to keep the apartment and all furnishings and have the lease and security deposit put in his/her name at discharge. But this proved to be too costly, and many youth could not afford the type of apartments where the state licensing authorities would permit us to house foster care youth.

We now help youth locate housing in areas where affordable apartments are located. We also make every attempt to facilitate the matching of youth being discharged who might be workable roommates.

What Seems to be Working in the Green Chimneys Program

Green Chimneys Life Skills program staff are inspired by the results of using the scattered-site apartment model and the residence model. The program has not had problems finding landlords willing to rent to the agency, and the geographical locations of our apartments allow clients to live in communities where they could afford to live after discharge. We have made every attempt to rent apartments and to site programs in neighborhoods that are diverse, affordable, and safe for our young people. The ability to move youth who do not act responsibly from apartments back to the Gramercy residence, or to group homes and foster homes, allows the program to give clients second chances and keep landlords happy.

The development of staff-resident relationships is another strength of the program. Relationships are probably the most important element of these programs, but also the most difficult to replicate.

How Success is Measured

In 1998, the agency conducted an outcome study and solicited the input of all former residents. Some of the salient findings from the study are reported below, organized according to six areas of client progress that we track.

1. Youth leaves the program with an affordable and potentially long-term place to stay.

Finding suitable and affordable living arrangements in New York City is challenging, even for those who have not spent time in out-of-home care. With studio apartments averaging $700 per month, young people exiting care used a variety of housing options. Forty-six percent of youth exiting care shared an apartment at discharge. Six months later, this figure increased to 51%. One of the more prominent findings was that a large proportion of youths (21%) returned to their families at discharge. We have also had moderate success in helping youth to enter subsidized housing situations.

2. Youth gained significant employment experience or vocational training.

Around 72% of our youth gain employment experience and leave placement with a full-time job.

Independence from reliance on public assistance is another indicator of economic self-sufficiency among youths discharged from our program. At discharge, only one young person in the study sample relied on public assistance as the sole means of financial support.

3. Youth made progress toward educational goals.

This has always been a program strength. Typically, about 74% of our clients make progress toward educational goals by leaving the program with a high school diploma or a GED. Twenty percent of youth leave the program with some college experience.

4. Youth's awareness of the need for savings has increased.

Closely linked to economic self-sufficiency is the ability to save one's earnings. A strength of the Green Chimneys program is its effectiveness in encouraging youths to open savings accounts. At discharge, 65% of the youth in our study sample had savings accounts, as compared with 4% who had one at intake. When asked what they most wished they had learned more about before leaving care, an overwhelming majority (90%) of respondents said they had difficulty budgeting their earnings and saving after discharge.

5. Youth's knowledge of independent living information has increased.

Youth are given a test on information related to independent living and self-sufficiency at entry, at discharge, and 6 months later at follow-up. Most do significantly better on the test at discharge and at follow-up than at entry.

6. Youth's overall sense of a support network was enhanced.

Approximately 96% of the youths discharged reported having at least one person in their life who provided a strong, close relationship. Sixty-seven percent of the discharged youths reported that they had regular contact with various individual staff members from the Green Chimneys Program and cited them as most helpful since their discharge.

Despite the positive outcomes reported above, most youths said that they found it harder than they expected to live independently. The two areas most frequently noted were the need to learn how to budget their money and the need for further education.

Our Most Common Problems with Clients

1. Youth who cannot motivate themselves to help themselves.

2. Youth who engage in substance abuse behavior.

3. Youth who engage in prostitution.

4. Youth who have hygiene problems.

5. Youth who have "issues" that they refuse to address with staff.

6. Youth who sabotage everything staff helps to set up for them.

7. Youth who don't sense the opportunities being offered.

8. Youth who actively avoid staff.

9. Damages caused by youth.

10. Youth who leave the program prematurely.

11. Youth who have more psychiatric/emotional problems than initially realized.

Things Staff Would Like to See Happen

- Extend the length of time for some youth, especially developmentally delayed and special needs youth.

- Terminate resistant youth and re-accept them when they are ready to go to work.

- Control the abundance of paperwork and paperwork requirements.

- Develop mentor relationships for all clients who want them.

- Spend more time with youth, especially more one-on-one attention.

- Establish emergency funds for former youth who run into trouble.

- Establish educational scholarships for youth in need.

- Locate more affordable housing options for former youth.

Most Common Staff-Related Problems

1. Low salaries for line workers.

2. Constant communication about daily activities is essential, but some-

times falls by the wayside.

3. Finding ways of dealing with the stress inherent in working with troubled adolescents.

4. Continuously changing and growing paperwork requirements.

5. Staff who avoid resistant, difficult, or needy youth.

6. Staff training in a diverse array of areas is essential.

7. Administrators sometimes have unrealistic expectations of line workers.

4

The Latin American Youth Center Transitional Living Program

Washington, D.C.

Aldo Hurtado

Brief History

The Latin American Youth Center (LAYC) is a community-based, multi-cultural, not-for-profit youth and family development organization founded in the late 1960s. The organization was incorporated as a 501(c)(3) in

1974 and has grown to an institution which today serves 5,000 youth and families. Situated at the heart of the Adams Morgan, Columbia Heights, and Mt. Pleasant neighborhoods of the District of Columbia, the LAYC serves the most ethnically diverse community in the District of Columbia. The LAYC has eight divisions: Educational Initiatives, Health Education, Community Services and Youth Leadership Development, Employment and Training, Arts and Recreation, YouthBuild, and Social Services. The LAYC's Transitional Living Program (TLP) for young men is part of LAYC's Social Services Division.

Description of the Program

The community surrounding the LAYC is predominantly an immigrant one, with a large number of families from Central and South America, Africa, the Caribbean, and Southeast Asia. Youth in this community are particularly at risk on a number of factors, including: substance abuse, gang involvement, risky sexual behavior, poverty, single-parent homes, violence, dropping out of school, and limited English proficiency.

These factors are exacerbated when a youth, in particular a young man, is not in a stable living environment. Large numbers of young men arrive in LAYC's community who are unaccompanied by families or guardians. When faced with homelessness and living on the streets, many immigrant young men are likely to become involved in drug trafficking, gangs, and other dangerous street activities.

For this reason, 6 years ago, taking advantage of a three-story house owned by the agency, the LAYC sought funding from the U.S. Department of Health and Human Services, Administration on Children, Youth and Families to develop and operate a TLP for boys. Since that time, the program has served over 80 young men between the ages of 16 and 21. The TLP provides a safe, home-like environment within a positive, community-based, supervised apartment-living setting. The program gives the young men an opportunity to take control of their lives by developing leadership, academic/vocational, and appropriate interaction skills in order to maintain positive relationships in the community, both in constructive leisure-time activities and in the work force. The philosophy of the TLP program is to involve youth in decisions that affect their lives in significant ways. For such a philosophy to crystallize, the youth must be ready to commit to the requirements of the program, which are detailed below.

Admission to the program requires three interviews: one with the TLP Case Manager, another with the LAYC clinical team, and the third with the Program Director. After this process is completed, the interviewers meet and decide whether the candidate is appropriate for the program.

Once admitted, the youth must be willing to go to school on a full- or part-time basis. In addition, he has to work on a part-time basis and open a savings account; he is required to deposit 25% of his monthly earnings into that account. The purpose of this requirement is to ensure that upon leaving the program, the youth will have enough cash to safely and easily make the transition to independent living.

In addition, the resident must be willing to participate in all other activities organized by the TLP, including (but not limited to) life skills classes, group and individual counseling, weekly meetings with his Case Manager, and biweekly house meetings.   Residents also have to clean the general living areas and their bedrooms every day. Finally, the youth must be willing to submit to random drug testing. Not abiding by these requirements may result in either suspension or termination from the program, depending on the degree and frequency of the violation. The same panel that served in the admission process serves in the quarterly case evaluation and discharge planning when needed.

Extensive efforts are made for the youth to be successful in the program.   Accordingly, the TLP staff makes sure that all services necessary to achieve self-sufficiency are provided. However, at times the TLP

Client Comment

"Many young people come to this country with goals in mind. Others are forced to immigrate because of their country's economical or political situation. I came to this country because of the two former issues.

Upon my arrival, the Transitional Living Program (TLP) helped me greatly in my life; the experience of living in a country where I struggle to achieve the best was eased by your presence and effective and timely intervention. The Street Outreach Program gave me a place to stay and friends whom I consider almost my brothers.

Prior to my admission to TLP, I was thinking about of dropping out of school and working full-time, but The TLP staff guided me and opened my eyes to the importance of education, and gave a chance to pursue my dreams.

Thank you very much TLP staff for all your support. As I go on with my life, I will always remember that in the midst of trouble and calamity you were there to give me a helping hand. I hope that you are there for other youth as you were for me.

Once again, I thank you from the bottom of my heart for the work you do and for giving young people the opportunity they need to continue pursuing our goals."

staff is forced to terminate a youth's participation in the program. There are several possible reasons for reaching such a decision.

The Latin American Youth Center does not tolerate violent behavior from participants or staff. Youth who actively engage in violent behavior are terminated from the program and immediately banned from the LAYC. There is a grievance process in place for those who wish to object to the decision. In the case of the TLP, so far we have had to terminate only one youth for violent behavior in the last 3 years.

A second reason for termination is the use or trafficking of illicit drugs. Upon admission, the residents are advised that drug use and/or distribution are not allowed in the program. As a matter of policy, the youth are subject to random drug screening and testing to ensure that every resident practices abstinence. Residents with positive drug results are required to participate in a drug-treatment program as well as AA/NA on a weekly basis. The TLP Case Manager, in collaboration with the LAYC treatment program, provides all needed referrals, and treatment participation is monitored by using a form signed weekly by the treatment provider(s). If the resident does not abide by these requirements, he is terminated within 7 days. This time allows the Case Manager to assist the youth in finding alternative housing. Drug trafficking in or around the building is not tolerated and subjects the youth to immediate termination.

Once in the program, the resident has to abide by a number of schedules, including cleaning his room and general living area twice a day, making required weekly deposits in his bank account, working and going to school, and observing his assigned curfew. In addition, he must participate in life skills and support groups on a weekly basis. Although occasional (or even repeated) non-compliance with one of these requirements will not result in expulsion, excessive or complete disregard for the program's rules and regulations will indeed result in dismissal from the program.

The youth may leave the program of his own accord if he decides that the program's goals are incongruent with his own. A youth, for instance, may want to work two jobs or go to school only. The program, however, requires that he work part-time and go to school full-time, or vice versa; he may not choose one over the other. In such cases, arrangements can be made for transfer to a program that meets the youth's particular goals.

Ordinarily, the TLP does not readmit a youth once he has been terminated from the program. The staff is always willing to work with the youth, however, for as long as it takes him to find an alternative living arrangement.

The TLP program has three phases. The completion of all requirements in each phase, plus the completion of each goal in the treatment plan, along with the subjective opinion of the resident, provide the staff with both quantitative and qualitative measures of the youth's success in the program.

Outline of Program Services

The LAYC TLP offers the following services:

Shelter. TLP assures that shelter is provided in a supervised living setting, with a staff ratio of 10 residents per full-time staff and 2 part-time staff, where residents are supervised 24 hours a day. The apartments are in a building within walking distance of the LAYC's administrative offices, where the majority of its programmatic services are located. The building is divided into two separate apartments, with administrative offices located in the basement. A three-bedroom apartment is the point of entry for all participants, who are expected to remain in that apartment for a maximum of 7 months. After the first 7 months, the participants move into a one-bedroom apartment located on the second floor, where they will spend 7-9 months before leaving the program. All housing is provided directly — no rent is charged to participants. In accordance with the Juvenile Justice and Delinquency Prevention Act (JJDPA), two of the primary goals of the TLP are to promote transition into self-sufficient living and to prevent long-term dependency on social services. The TLP has tailored its services to meet these goals.

One of the most important elements of TLP is Life Skills. The Life Skills curriculum (described in more detail below) provides residents with the necessary skills to survive on their own. They are taught to find and retain employment, balance their savings account, hygiene, etc. Completion of the Life Skills curriculum, coupled with the working and savings requirement of the program, ensures that in 12-18 months the residents will be able to make an easy transition from the TLP to living independently.

In 1 year, youth usually have saved enough money to rent their own place and have internalized the value of saving well enough that they seldom need our assistance after a planned discharge.

Once a resident exhausts his time in the program, a meeting is called with the youth and all parties involved in the case to make arrangements for discharge and a 6-month follow-up. The TLP Case Manager, in coordination with the youth and his counselor, develops a monthly budget for the youth and assists him in finding a safe and affordable living arrangement.

Independent Living Skills. For young men, adolescence marks a time filled with changes and choices. Complex decisions and the challenges of growing up make the teenage years difficult. This situation is more critical for homeless and runaway youth, who are at high risk for getting involved in criminal activities. In this context, TLP residents must learn skills necessary to function well in society. The TLP uses an Independent Living Skills Program curriculum developed by the program to help its participants learn these skills. The young men participate in lessons concerning communication, health and sexuality, hygiene, grooming and personal appearance, housing, community resource utilization, transportation, menu planning and food management, banking and money management, housekeeping, leisure-time activities, consumer education, homemaking skills, and employment searching and retaining skills.

As mentioned above, the LAYC is divided into eight divisions, each specialized in an area such as employment, health, counseling, or recreation. To effectively address the needs of the TLP residents and to meet the goals of our Life Skills curriculum, the TLP relies on the LAYC divisions. Members of the LAYC staff take turns in teaching a specific area of Life Skills, according to their expertise. Hence, the TLP youth are taught by the members of the LAYC staff most knowledgeable about, and hired to deal with, a given issue. The Life Skills class is taught once per week, for 1 hour at a time. To ensure that the youth are learning the material, the program relies on questionnaires that provide both quantitative and qualitative data. Such information, in turn, allows the staff member to assess the effectiveness of the sessions and to evaluate his/her own work.

The TLP Life Skills curriculum is a dynamic one that permits the staff to make changes according to the needs and observations of the ever-changing TLP group.

Group Counseling. Group interventions are used to create a mutual support system. The main goals are to provide an opportunity for members to learn assertiveness skills and practice their application to real life situations, to expand awareness of one's own behavior, to learn positive ways to express thoughts and feelings to others, to develop trust in one's own judgment, and to relate to adults and peers with increased awareness and effective communication. Like the Life Skills class, group counseling is a once-a-week, 1-hour session.

Educational Advancement. Each participant is required to enroll in an educational program during the first 2 weeks in the program. New residents meet individually with the Case Manager and Career Developer to discuss their educational options. This gives residents time to think about immediate actions while the staff gathers school information, diagnoses educational needs, and makes appropriate school referral appointments.

Educational services also include referrals to alternative programs such as GED preparation, English as a Second Language, and vocational/training programs. The staff maintains close ties with guidance counselors and teachers at the neighboring schools attended by TLP residents. When family members are not available, the Case Manager attends parent-teacher conferences and acts as an advocate for the resident. The program offers each participant the opportunity to work with volunteer tutors on a one-to-one basis.

In addition, the LAYC has recently opened a public charter school, the Next Step, which offers GED and ESL programs to young people who have dropped out of traditional public schools. The LAYC also operates a YouthBuild Program, a national model for increasing housing stock for homeless and low-income residents while providing education, as well as leadership and construction skills training to young people. Both the Next Step Public Charter School and the YouthBuild Program are available to TLP residents.

Job Preparation and Attainment. Although part of the Life Skills curriculum, the employment aspect of the TLP is so vast and the need so great that it could be seen as an independent service category. New residents follow a series of steps in exploring job opportunities. Many hours are spent instructing the participants in job readiness, both during the Life Skills hours and beyond. The areas discussed include appropriate dress for job interviews, how to fill out job applications, how and where to look for employment, and the job interview process. TLP residents are referred to the LAYC Employment and Training Division. There they are assigned a caseworker, whose responsibility is to help them find and retain a job.

Health and Psychosocial Assessments. Upon arrival, new residents are referred to local health clinics for physical examinations. The LAYC, in conjunction with two community health centers, operates an adolescent health clinic where TLP residents can go and receive services in a culturally sensitive setting.

The purpose of the psychosocial assessment is to identify and analyze the cause(s) of the resident's housing situation and to implement effective interventions. Based on the assessment, the counselor will work with each resident to improve his psychosocial functioning in all areas of daily activity.

Drug Abuse Prevention and Treatment. This program includes individual and group counseling interventions provided through the certified staff of the LAYC Social Service Division drug-treatment program.

Through the group process-learning model applied to recovery principles, the focus of the counseling activities is to continuously present the individual with the challenge to overcome denial and accept the need to take responsibility for modifying his behavior.

Food. The TLP provides food to all residents during their stay in the program. A cook is on staff to help youth learn to prepare food four times a week. Under the supervision of a staff person, and to put into practice what was learned during the week, one resident is required to cook on the weekend for his peers. In this way, participants learn about nutrition and how to prepare meals on a budget, at both the theoretical and practical levels. The food subsidy is gradually reduced as residents begin progressing into the advanced phases of the program.

Case Management. The primary goal of case management is to maximize the resident's functioning and development of his potential, which includes problem-solving and coping capacities. The Case Manager acts as facilitator to help residents define their goals and to make resources accessible to their needs.

Outreach. The LAYC has an extensive outreach system that includes: 1) LAYC's drop-in recreation center, which serves approximately 100 young people daily and acts as a point of entry for many new arrivals in the District's Latino community; 2) a Street Outreach Program that employs Youth Outreach Workers, who spend many hours canvassing community streets identifying at-risk youth and integrating them into LAYC programs; and 3) referrals from community agencies, schools, and churches.

Our Five Most Common Problems

1. Twenty percent of the population served is undocumented. The provision of services outside the LAYC for such youth is minimal, but extraordinarily necessary.

2. Dysfunctional youth forming alliances with other youth in the program and coercing them into being equally disruptive.

3. Limited space relative to the demand for housing.

4. Difficulties accessing immediate medical assistance for youth.

5. Getting youth to save 25% of their total monthly earnings.

Things Staff Would Like to See Happen

- A full-time Career Counselor.

- A building designed to support full program activities.

- Additional funding for more extracurricular activities and technical support.

- More police involvement in the community.

- A larger budget to make it possible for the program to provide all the services that the youth need, as well as to help the program compete more successfully for staff with better paying positions available to staff outside of the District.

Other Latin American Youth Center Residential Programs

The LAYC TLP program operates in conjunction with several other LAYC residential programs. These programs cover a wide variety of services, ranging from emergency housing to long-term transitional housing. The LAYC strives to create a network of services that ensures that all youth who come to it in need can be offered help. The additional LAYC programs include:

Foster Care Program — The LAYC is a licensed foster care agency in the District of Columbia and Virginia. LAYC trains and licenses Latino families to become foster care parents. It licenses culturally and language appropriate foster homes for the placement of Latino youth entering the child welfare system.

Street Outreach Program (SOP) — The SOP provides emergency housing and case management for runaway and homeless youth. This program is operated out of a facility owned by the LAYC.

Host Home Program — The Host Home Program provides short-term (15 days) residential assistance and case management to girls who find themselves homeless. Many of the girls in this program have babies and, therefore, cannot be placed in foster care placements. Participants in the Host Home Program are placed in private homes in the community. Most of the hosts have gone through LAYC's foster care training. Hosts are paid through a Basic Center HHS grant; the girls themselves do not pay their hosts. Girls in this program must abide by the LAYC code of conduct. In addition, the case worker sets out specific rules for each girl. After leaving the host home, some girls are reunited with their families, some go on to independent living, and some are placed in other programs. The main problem faced by this program is finding a constant supply of hosts.

Latino Transitional Housing Program — This HUD-funded program is run by the Council of Latino Agencies in Washington, D.C. in conjunction with several other community agencies, including LAYC. It provides transitional housing (18 months) and case management to girls over the age of 18 who are runaway or homeless. The program pays for participants to rent apartments in the community. Roommate situations are set up only in emergencies. The main problem for this program has been finding affordable housing.

Long-Term Program Development

In July 1998, the LAYC completed the purchase, renovation, and furnishing of its new administrative and program facility, consolidating six scattered unsafe facilities to one central location. That capital campaign, a 3-year project, is considered a model of success by many local organizations. With that experience successfully completed, the LAYC is undertaking the renovation of four houses around the corner from the LAYC administrative offices. This renovation project is intended to expand and improve LAYC's current residential services. The project aims to refurbish the building where the TLP is currently located, as well as to renovate the other buildings to create a TLP for runaway and homeless girls and teenage mothers and their babies. LAYC's goal is to raise $1,000,000 for this effort. This would include the purchase, renovation, and furnishing of the three additional buildings.

Dealing with the TLP Residents' Families

In general, the community has welcomed the LAYC initiative to create and implement a Transitional Living Program for Youth. New immigrants and the disadvantaged see the TLP as a gateway to opportunities that they would not have otherwise. The positive perception that the community has of the LAYC in general, and the TLP in particular, creates an atmosphere of trust and cooperation between the TLP staff, the residents, and their families.

The TLP residents may be visited by family members every day until 9:00 p.m. In addition, the staff is always available to discuss any concerns that parents may have regarding the program and/or the youth. Once per month, the residents are allowed to spend the night outside the TLP house. Most of them choose to spend that time with their families. This latter fact is indicative of, and a vehicle for, reestablishing good familial relations.

Client Comment

"I am going to start my letter by referring you to the African proverb 'It takes a Village to raise a Child.' Like many young men and women of my age, growing up in these modern times is so difficult. Our families are failing us, friends are deserting us and we are left alone to make our daily choices all by ourselves. More often we are too naïve and young to make the right decisions, hence most of the decisions we make often end up affecting our future, either bad or good. At times like these, we need the 'Village' to rescue us.

This is where the Transitional Program (TLP) comes in; it was my last hope. I was born in Lagos, Nigeria. My parents were a typically middle class people. They had been separated before I celebrated my first birthday. Growing up for me was difficult and mostly lonesome. My mom had her own business and my dad lived mostly overseas and both of them seldom had time to raise me. I had to live my life on school campuses, with uncles, aunt and mostly my step mom. As a matter of fact, my family had lost a grip of me at a tender age.

By my teenage years, I moved to the United States to live with my dad. The situation just got worse chronologically. My happiness was like a thing I could only have in my dreams. Finally a couple of months after my high school graduation, I left my dad's house in search of a more promising future. TLP was just the right place for me; I wanted to live a better, more successful and happier life. It was like I had a new family, I woke up in the morning and I could talk to anybody about how I felt. I had counselors, case managers and tutors who made sure my life went smooth. Then I started excelling in everything I did.

As of today, I have graduated from the TLP program. While I was in the program, I saved enough money to get my own place. I went on to college (University of the District of Columbia), and come next fall I am starting the school year as a junior majoring in computer science. I have also received scholarship such as 'Community Impact Scholarship' two years in a row. I also have a full time job and a school cumulative GPA of 3.375. Everything I have done so far comes as a result of the investment, which the TLP made in me. TLP was my last resource and my own 'Village' which came to my rescue. I sincerely extend my gratitude to you and everybody at TLP for the help you have rendered. I can only hope that you and your crew continue to change the life of the more young people that are still going to walk into your door."

5

Franklin County Children Services Emancipation Department

Grove City, Ohio

Diann Stevens

Brief History

Franklin County Children Services, a public county entity, began its formal commitment to the Emancipation/Independent Living programming in February 1983, following an extensive in-house assessment of the type and depth of adult readiness services being provided to the Children Services adolescent caseload. Children Services learned through the final study report that, although individual social workers and specific adolescent units addressed these issues in their general planning for teens, no formal, organized, and nationally researched Independent Living programming existed.

Franklin County Children Services fully concurred with the then-emerging national concern that too many teens were exiting from the foster care system ill prepared to assume their roles as productive adults of the community. Recognizing that preparation for successful adult independence is a lifelong process, Children Services, through the creation of the Emancipation Department, began an extensive in-depth development and implementation process designed to put in place in the Agency a multifaceted, flexible, realistic Independent Living program.

Five basic philosophical commitments guided this program development:

1. Children have a right to a safe and secure childhood;

2. Child welfare youth have usually been denied this basic right;

3. All youth, regardless of competencies, will join and participate in the adult community successfully or unsuccessfully;

4. Youth have the right to be treated with respect and dignity, regardless of the family or personal problems that brought them to the child welfare system;

5. All adults and systems interacting with a youth have the professional, moral, and ethical responsibility to be positive role models for and facilitators of those youth in learning how to become independent.

Description of the Emancipation Department

Outline of Services

Children Services provides the following mandated services: Prevention, Protection, Foster Care, Adoptions, Intake and Investigation, Volunteer and Mentor Services. In addition, Children Services has developed the following continuum of services for youth involved in the emancipation process:

- Assessment/Case Planning
- Adult Life Skills Training
- Employment Counseling
- Transitional Living Program
- Host Homes
- Independent Living Program
- Annual Teen Conference

Assessment/case planning. All youth 16 years and older and active on the Children Services caseload are eligible for emancipation services. The specific program area and intensity of services are dependent on the needs of the youth and the resources of the department and agency.

Youth referred to the department are assigned an emancipation counselor and participate in an assessment and planning experience that sets the emancipation plan in place. Also involved in this planning process are the youth's social worker, parent, foster parent or any caregiver, and mentor, as well as anyone else centrally involved in the youth's life and development.

Adult Life Skills training. The Emancipation Department provides a 10-week formal life skills training curriculum designed by Franklin County staff and conducted by the in-house life skills coordinator. All youth referred are eligible for this experience, but it is a requirement for youth progressing to one of our housing options.

Areas covered include, but are not limited to: employment, banking/taxes, budgeting, consumer awareness, self-esteem, and personal hygiene.

Employment counseling. Employment is essential for successful independence. The Emancipation Department provides employment counseling to youth that aims at identifying current skills and areas of interest, building self-confidence, and assisting youth in obtaining employment opportunities.

Transitional Living Program. In order to begin the realistic practice of what will actually be expected of youth when they enter the adult community, a program has been developed to provide *steps* into that reality.

Transitional Living is a semi-supervised youth living situation, with five locations across Columbus, where staff members are on site from 7 p.m. to 8 a.m. Franklin County Children Services' Transitional Living Program serves young people from the age of 17+.

The Emancipation Department has developed a relationship with three local landlords who work specifically with our Transitional Living locations. Two have been involved with the program since its inception, and the other came on board during 1999. These landlords are very familiar with the goals of the program and have even presented about their role at state conferences. They know when to call staff and when a particular youth has been given enough chances and is not responding to staff or landlord requests for more responsible behavior.

The agency is able to move youth in and out of different sites as needed in Transitional Living. The landlords meet all new youth and give them their first experience interacting with a real-life landlord. The youth find out immediately that these landlords know the program rules and expectations and will not hesitate to report a rules infraction.

During the day, youth are expected to work on employment and educational goals. A staff member floats from site to site to monitor youth activities during the hours of 8 a.m. to 5 p.m. The adult staff members serve as resident mentor counselors and facilitate the learning of both tangible and intangible skills.

Youth share an apartment and/or rooming house, manage their own monies, and take responsibility for their own choices and decisions. Youth have this experience while trained professionals are still there to assist, guide, and provide a listening ear.

Youth receive a monthly stipend for participating in the Transitional Living Program and, in turn, use these stipend monies, plus any from their own employment, to pay monthly living costs. Youth remain in this program for approximately 4 to 6 months, and sometimes longer, before moving on to an actual independent living apartment.

Host homes. The Department uses host homes on occasion to provide an independent living experience for our youth aged 16 years and over. A host home is a living arrangement whereby a non-relative agrees to rent a room to a youth. The adult's role is to provide independent living training to the youth. Adults serve more as mentors than parents. Youth living in host homes receive a monthly stipend of $512 to cover their rent.

Independent Living Program scattered-site apartments. We learned early on that teaching independent living skills is not enough. Youth must also have the opportunity to practice what they have been taught. In response, Children Services started the Scattered-Site Independent Living Program in 1987. Children Services assists youth in establishing themselves in an appropriate community setting.

As program participants, these youth receive stipend dollars, as well as income from any employment, to pay for their monthly expenses. The amount of the monthly stipend is based on such living expenses as rent and utilities. Stipends range from $512 - $750.

The Emancipation Department assists youth in securing employment and housing, setting up a budget, shopping, and with all of the anticipated fears and adjustments people face when they go out on their own.

Budgets are designed so that, as the months progress, youth assume more and more of the expenses from their employment income and less from their stipend check. The goal is that Children Services will motivate youth to become financially independent several months before their case is closed.

Youth assume responsibility for their lives as their independent living competencies grow. *The setting is designed to allow learning experiences and normal mistakes while youth are still under the care of the agency.*

Potential Problems with the IL Scattered-Site Program

Independent living is seen as the least restrictive living arrangement that can be offered to youth in child welfare. From residential settings, foster care, group homes, to independent living, there are always questions regarding risk and liability. The young person is held to the same standards as any other adult living in the community. Many people are fearful that youth might break the law or cause some other problems living on their own. However, in most instances, youth are *very* responsible, because they come to realize that they are destroying their own property and putting themselves in jeopardy by participating in risky behavior. Reality is the key when attempting to give knowledge to these young people. If they break the law, natural consequences follow, such as eviction, payment for damages, or incarceration.

Constant communication with the youth, parents, employer, landlord, and school personnel helps to lessen the opportunities for the youth to get into trouble. It is important for everyone to be "on the same page."

Average Daily Population

Our average daily population is approximately 80 young people in all of our living situations. This does not include about 50 young people who are enrolled in the Adult Life Skills classes only.

We do not routinely serve youth from the correctional system. We do serve some youth who have had involvement with the juvenile court system, but we usually do not accept anyone with a previous serious felony offense.

Staff Roles

The Department consists of 6 social workers whose working title is Emancipation Counselor, 1 Transitional Living Supervisor, 2 Transitional Living Coordinators, and 29 community-based Resident Mentors who work one-to-one with the youth in Transitional Living.

Emancipation Counselors provide direct services to youth preparing for emancipation. They assist youth in locating housing, developing budgets, securing employment, and/or completing educational experiences. They also provide weekly counseling, monitoring, and evaluation.

The Transitional Living Supervisor provides guidance and supervision to the Transitional Living Coordinators and the 29 community-based Resident Mentors, who work one-to-one directly with the youth in Transitional Living. The Transitional Living Coordinators provide direct supervision to the Resident Mentors, while also providing the first line of contact with the youth in Transitional Living.

Client emergency calls are handled through our agency's 24-hour hot line. Two staff members are on 24-hour call daily. If they can't handle the emergency, they contact the youth's Emancipation Counselor or family social worker, if one is involved.

It is important to select staff who are not afraid of teens. They must also believe in the philosophical concepts behind emancipation and independent living. We select staff who believe that these young people must be properly trained for life on their own, that we are their guardians, and that therefore it is our responsibility to teach them.

Geographical Range — Areas Served

The Emancipation Department serves youth involved with Franklin County Children Services. We generally cover the city of Columbus and some surrounding locations within Franklin County.

Funding

The department is funded by agency local tax levy dollars and the Federal Independent Living Initiative. The cost of independent living is much less in comparison to the cost of most residential institutions and group homes. The agency has saved an average of $2 million annually with independent living, compared to the costs of other placement options.

Client Involvement in Program Development

Youth are involved in their case planning from the very beginning, starting with the assessment process. They have the opportunity to express their opinions, thoughts, goals, and objectives. These are incorporated into the Emancipation Case Plan, which is the road map for the youth's stay in the program. The plan is reviewed periodically at staffing meetings to assess the youth's progress, or lack thereof. If necessary, new plans are developed.

Problems Specific to Each Housing Option

Scattered-site apartments. The basic problem with this option is finding and retaining landlords who will rent to youth under the age of 18. Once they have tried the program, they usually stick with it, sometimes setting aside a number of apartments for our youth.

Transitional Living houses. It is extremely important to watch the mix of youth in the house. Staff must properly screen for personality disorders, cultural issues, and self-esteem issues. Youth need to feel independent, while also being aware of the interaction in the house.

In terms of selecting a location for a transitional home, we attempt to keep a low profile in the neighborhood so as not to draw any NIMBY (Not In My Back Yard) responses. Where necessary, we introduce ourselves to the neighbors and convince them that we will be on top of everything that goes on in the home. We also give our closest neighbors our office and pager numbers for emergency contacts. In addition, we introduce our-selves to law enforcement personnel in the area.

Generally, once a youth is accepted into the Emancipation Department, there is no return to paid/structured placement. We can move a youth from a scattered-site apartment to transitional living, to host home and back, but that is about the extent to which we currently utilize our housing continuum.

Children Services is a public agency that usually holds custody of the youth. Therefore, there are very few terminations from the scattered-site program unless, of course, a youth breaks the law and enters the state cor-rectional system. Terminations do not usually occur unless the youth is 18 years of age or older. Reasons for termination would include failure to work or attend school and/or an ongoing failure to follow program rules.

Who Signs the Lease and Why?

Franklin County Children Services does not sign the leases on any of the property used for Transitional or Independent Living. The youth sign all leases. This gives the youth the experience of interacting with the rental agent/landlord. The rental agents/landlords agree with this process, know-ing that the lease is not enforceable. We have a working relationship with them; they know that for the length of the lease (6 months - a year) their rent will be paid.

Liability/Risk Management Issues

Liability issues are handled as they would be with any other renter in the community. The landlord looks to the tenant as the person responsible for any damages. We usually work out any large damages with the landlord or rental agent. Security deposits are kept in other instances. Although we have had some instances of expensive repair bills, we usually look to the youth to cover them or face charges.

What Seems to be Working

A major success for the program has been at the systems level. IL is now a major part of the county agency placement continuum. It is no longer seen as an add-on, luxury service but as part of the comprehensive services offered by our county.

The department's staff retention and stability are excellent, and with our low staff turnover, the experience gained by staff with each youth only enhances the services received by the next youth. The stability of our staff is a result of job satisfaction and increased involvement with the youth. Staff also cite the sense of accomplishment they feel when one youth completes his/her plan and moves on with life as a major reason they remain in this field.

How Success is Measured

It is hard to measure success with the youth we serve. The transient nature of their lifestyle makes it difficult. Franklin County Children Services, in most cases, continues to work with youth past the age of 18 to better insure success. We don't cut participants off at 18 years; we try to support youth at least 6 months past their 18th birthday. Once they leave the system, it is hard to keep in touch with them unless they want to.

We see high school graduation as an important measure of success, but for some of our youth it is not possible. Many are several years behind as they approach age 18 and would not realistically graduate until they reach 20 or 21 years. We work hard to see that clients receive at least a GED if possible. Some of our clients do not pass a GED test or state proficiency test because of cognitive limitations or learning disabilities.

Maintaining employment is critical to the youths' success. For these youth, maintaining a job for 6 months is seen as a major victory. Many of them leave the program with established jobs in place.

Some Typical Rules and Policies

There are to be no overnight guests. Pets are allowed if the housing authority or apartment complex allows them. Our only requirement is that the pet be properly taken care of; for example, they need to have a veterinarian. We do not pay for "extras" like cable TV, recreation, or cigarettes. We call that "get a job" (smile). We do not provide an allowance. For risk/liability reasons, we also do not sign for driver's licenses. The client usually obtains a license upon reaching the age of 18.

Our Top Ten Most Common Problems

1. Family members who move in with the youth in their apartments.

2. Friends who try to move in.

3. Apartment break-ins (usually the youth's friends).

4. Loud music and noise.

5. Too many visitors.

6. Lack of follow-through by youth.

7. Unemployability of youth.

8. Apartment damage.

9. Youth who sabotage their plan until they realize their case is closing, and then we become the bad guys.

10. Increasing number of delinquent and unruly youth.

Things Staff Would Like to See Happen

■ A structured aftercare program.

■ More team meetings with other agencies involved with the youth, i.e., MRDD, Mental Health.

Most Common Staff-Related Problems

One of the biggest problems for staff is poor client motivation. Most of these young adults have been part of the child welfare system for many years, and they feel they are entitled to be "cared for" instead of learning to care for themselves. In most cases they do not realize the seriousness of the learning process until it is too late, i.e., custody is terminated and/or their case is about to be closed. Also, the client base is becoming more problematic. We must plan for the more severely abused, unruly, and delinquent client. This calls for greater staff creativity in terms of housing and monitoring.

More Information

Acceptance in the Community

In general terms, we are well accepted in the community. There are always those few parents who feel we are creating more problems than we are solving. Some parents, who have put their child out of the home, then want to tell us how to handle the case. Also, they expect us to "fix" what they could not. Our feeling in the department is that, if you can meet with the community (especially neighbors) to explain the program philosophy and concept, there is a greater chance they will be accepting.

6

The Lighthouse Youth Services Independent Living Program

Cincinnati, Ohio

Mark J. Kroner

Brief History

The Lighthouse Independent Living Program (ILP) was established in 1981 in response to an obvious community need. Agency staff knew that many of the older youth leaving our group homes, foster homes, and shelters were not able to return to their families' homes for numerous reasons. These youth frequently called agency staff a few weeks, and sometimes just days, after leaving the child welfare system, saying that they had no place to live. The county agreed to a proposal made by Bob Mecum, the agency Executive Director, to allow us to try placing youth in apartments around the community and provide financial assistance, case management, and support services to youth for several months *before* they were discharged from the system.

Over the years, this private/public collaboration has proven to be a valuable addition to the continuum of care for high-risk youth in Hamilton County, Ohio. As of 1999, the Program has served over 600 youth, many of whom have gone on to become productive and responsible community members. Some of our former clients continue to work with the program in various training, mentoring, and advocacy roles.

The program serves youth ages 16-19 in custody of a county children's services or juvenile corrections system. The program also serves youth exiting state correctional facilities. In addition, the agency operates a Transitional Living Program (TLP) for "non-systems youth," i.e., young adults ages 18-22 who are not in the care of any system. Most of these clients are referred from the adult homeless shelter system. Although some TLP clients were formerly in county custody, very few were previously in an independent living program. The TLP is funded with Federal Runaway and Homeless Youth Act funds, HUD funds, state grants, and donations. Staff from the ILP and TLP interact frequently and act as resources to each other. As of this writing, the Lighthouse Transitional Living Program has served over 300 young adults. This chapter, however, will focus solely on the services for youth still in custody.

Description of the Program

The Lighthouse ILP utilizes primarily the scattered-site apartment model. This model seems to work best in terms of client ownership of responsibility, limiting group control issues, geographical flexibility, and cost. The agency also owns two shared homes, small houses with three beds for clients and either a live-in staff member or "awake" overnight staff. Youth in rural areas are sometimes placed in "host homes," essentially sharing the house of an adult or married couple. The agency also is able to place females in a large boarding home in the downtown area. Various roommate situations have been attempted with mixed success. Allowing ILP clients to share an apartment with a non-client has worked better than two clients sharing an apartment.

Lighthouse Independent Living Program Objectives

1. To provide housing, supervision, and financial assistance to youth who

are in need of these services to prepare them for independent functioning when they are emancipated.

2. To provide intensive training in skills, knowledge, and information needed to function independently in the community.

3. To provide "real life" experience in independent living, allowing youth to learn by doing while being supervised by trained staff.

4. To provide emotional support, crisis counseling, and guidance to youth in the program.

5. To assist youth in finding and maintaining employment in the community.

6. To assist other programs and agencies in the community in preparing youth for independent living.

7. To make every effort possible to assure that clients exit care with a safe and affordable place to live.

Outline of Program Services

Housing. Youth are assisted in locating and moving into an apartment in a neighborhood that suits their needs. Apartments are equipped with used and donated furnishings and all basic supplies. The program signs the lease and pays the security deposit. Roommate situations can happen but usually do not work out. Non-client roommates have been tried with some success. Youth are able to keep the apartment and all furnishings and supplies if they have a source of income at discharge and have proven to the landlord that they are responsible.

Financial support. The agency covers rent, utilities (up to $40 a month), and phone bills (toll blocks prevent long distance calls). Youth often take over one or several bills during the last few months in the program. Clients receive a weekly allowance of $45 for food, transportation, laundry, and personal items. Another $15 is put in an agency savings account each week, and the total minus any damages is released to youth at discharge. Clients with jobs can live off what they make and have their entire $60 per month placed in savings. Some youth leave the program and the system with significant savings.

Life skills training. All participants have the opportunity to work on a 24-project life skills training curriculum at their own pace. Their assigned social worker gives them project requirements, and, if all 24 components are completed, the youth earns $300. Youth who are busy with school and work often do not complete their life skills training, but usually already know most of the information.

Emotional support/guidance. Each youth is assigned a social worker with an average caseload of 10-12 youth, as well as an Independent Living Specialist who works with two or more social workers. Social workers see youths weekly at the ILP office or at the youth's apartment. Specialists also visit apartments and are involved in connecting youth to community resources. ILP staff members are on-call 24/7 every 9 weeks. Staff provide informal counseling around daily living issues, and all staff assist clients with numerous types of crises. Youth not working or going to school attend weekly support groups run by the agency psychologist. Attempts are made to connect clients to any family, relative, or other supports.

Case management/planning. Participants are connected to schools, jobs, vocational training, therapists, AA meetings, sex-offenders groups, parenting classes, or whatever community service is needed. Frequent meetings with caseworkers are held to review progress. All activities are geared to prepare the youth for life after the child welfare system.

Outreach. The program is involved in ongoing outreach efforts that include weekend self-sufficiency workshops, foster parent training, training and consultation to other caregivers, involvement in local, state, and national coalitions, and dissemination of training materials. A yearly, city-wide conference on Self-Sufficiency and Independent Living gathers foster parents, youth, probation officers, social workers, former clients, and other care-providers to discuss the needs of youth leaving care. The program director is continuously networking and meeting with local providers to discuss program development.

Average Daily Population

Currently, the average daily population is around 45-50 youth. Between 1981 and 1997, we averaged around 18 youth a day. A managed-care arrangement, which started in January, 1998, resulted in a sharp increase in referrals. The managed-care staff realized early on that the IL services were less expensive than group homes, residential treatment, or therapeutic foster care. They also noticed that many youth did better living alone than in group or family settings. Overall, they liked the ILP's focus on self-sufficiency and exiting the system from a furnished apartment in which they lived before discharge.

Geographical Range — Areas Served

Youth are placed primarily in our county, but they can be placed as far as 50 miles from the ILP office. Most clients live within a five-mile range of our office.

Staffing

Position	*Responsibilities*
Program Director	Oversees program services, staff, and budget; Involved in community networking, program development, grant writing, training, and public relations; Supervises staff development and program quality assurance.
Assistant Director	Interviews potential clients; Oversees case-management process; Trouble shoots client and staff problems; Assigned program development activities by director; Supervises social workers and IL specialists.
5 Full-time Social Workers	Oversee client progress and case-management activities; Responsible for documentation and record keeping; Communicate with referring agency, parent, court system, etc.; Deal with landlords, referring agency caseworkers, and families.
2-3 IL Specialists	Assist social workers with case-management activities; Help find apartments for clients and oversee moves; Help monitor and supervise clients; Help with client transports and appointments; Facilitate life skills training process.
Full-time Office Manager	Serves as the communications hub of the program; Oversees billing, record keeping, file maintenance; Interfaces with agency Management Information System and accounting staff.
Student Interns	Guide clients through life skills projects; Assist with moves and supervision; Serve as mentors and case aides.

Life Coaches	Assigned to MRDD and special needs youth; Visit assigned clients daily; Provide transportation and teach life skills.
Clinical Supervisor (part-time with ILP)	Conducts bimonthly clinical case review; Conducts weekly client support groups for youth not yet productively occupied.

Funding Sources

- Per diem contracts with local children's services and juvenile courts (using primary local tax dollars).

- Title IV-E IL funds for training.

- State competitive discretionary grants.

- Federal demonstration grants.

- Private donations.

- Client income (minor).

- Agency fund-raising efforts.

Staff Comment

"Most of our youth stay about a year in the program. But we've had a number run away from their own fully furnished apartments with all of their bills paid. I always wonder what they ran to. One very successful client told us after she left she wanted to hitchhike to the West Coast. She eventually called us from Haight-Ashbury — wisely we convinced her to let us hang on to some of her money."

Assessment of Client Strengths and Needs

This is an ongoing process that involves feedback from the youth, referring agency caseworker, previous caregivers, a written test on IL information (created by the program), and a behavioral checklist (also program-created).

Life Skills Training Strategies

Life skills are taught in several ways in our county. We are attempting to get all youth 16 and older through a self-sufficiency training program offered on Saturdays from 10 a.m.-3 p.m. Youth receive $10 for completing the 13-week course and receive $30 after completing all 13 sessions. Week-long, all-day self-sufficiency "camps" are held in the summer for groups of 10-15. This training opportunity involves lectures, videos, games, group and individual exercises, guest speakers, and former ILP clients. Youth who attend and participate all week receive $100 (which comes from Title IV-E Federal IL Initiative funds). Once youth enter our apartment program, they can complete a 24-project basic life skills curriculum at their own pace.

Client Involvement in Program Development

Ideally, youth referred to the Lighthouse ILP have been involved in the county self-sufficiency program and have been given enough time to think about and plan for their stay in the ILP. Youth often initiate the process by asking their county caseworker if they can be considered for the program. Occasionally a meeting is held with the ILP director while the youth is still in foster or group care to discuss what the youth would need to do to be referred to the ILP. Once accepted, youth can help find their own living arrangement and help plan the move. The program respects the youth's input on the best overall plan of action concerning choice of school, neighborhood, proximity to social supports, and the cultural appropriateness of the apartment. Within 30 days of placement, the youth, his/her caseworker, the assigned ILP social worker, and other involved parties meet to develop an individualized service plan. Parents are invited, in writing, to attend this meeting.

Staff Comment

"I recently received a call from a former client who entered our program at age 16. She really had a tough time while in the ILP. I couldn't imagine how she could make it alone. Well, now at age 23 she just bought a house and has the same job that one of our team helped her find. She's now a supervisor and makes more than many of us!"

Types of Housing Options Utilized by the Lighthouse ILP

Most of our youth live in individual scattered-site apartments. We have two shared homes with three beds each, one for males and one for females. A staff person lives in the females' house, and we have awake staff on duty overnight in the male shared home. Occasionally we place a youth in a host home, i.e., the house of an adult or couple with a room available. We also have access to a boarding home in our city center for young adult women who need more supervision (there is 24-hour staffing) or have been evicted from a previous living arrangement. Sometimes youth are placed in roommate situations with youth who are not in the system, e.g., a good friend who is moving out of his/her family home. Youth who are leaving the program without full-time jobs in place are put on a low-income housing company waiting list and moved into subsidized apartments when their names come up.

Descriptions of Current Lighthouse Housing Options

- Individual scattered-site apartments — apartments throughout the area owned by private landlords.

- Shared homes — houses owned by the agency with four beds, one for a resident manager and three for program participants.

- Host homes — arrangements in which a youth lives with an adult or married couple in the adult's or couple's house.

- Boarding homes — youth lives in a room in a large SRO (single room occupancy) building owned and run by another social service agency.

- Roommate situations — various situations in which a program participant and another youth share a one- or two-bedroom apartment. The roommate can be a non-systems youth.

- Subsidized housing — an apartment rented by the participant from an agency overseeing low-income housing units.

Staff Comment

"There is no correlation between intelligence and success in the ILP. We have clients with IQs of 70 who are doing great and whiz kids who can't get through a day without breaking someone's rules or windows. There is a correlation between common sense and success."

Throughout their stay in the ILP, clients are able to assess their ability to maintain their current living arrangement. Before a client's next-to-last month in the program, ILP social workers usually discuss the feasibility of remaining in the current situation or other options available to the client. If necessary, the program assists the client in moving into another more affordable or more convenient location.

If a client is not capable of living on his/her own, the ILP staff does everything possible to assure that the client finds a workable, affordable situation upon discharge. The agency is continually developing living arrangement options for the clients of this community.

The Independent Living Program assesses referred youth through the intake process, which includes a review of social and psychological histories, conversations with caseworkers, a written life skills assessment, and a face-to-face interview between the youth and caseworker. From this process the ILP determines a living arrangement appropriate to the youth's level of functioning and the level of staff involvement needed. The length of time the youth has to remain in the ILP determines much about the location of placement and the individualized plan for independent living.

Cost of Various Housing Options

We receive a basic rate of $55-60 per day per client with increases for special-needs clients. The program does not change the per diem when a living arrangement changes. The program requires additional funds for youth with special needs who need daily staff contact.

Problems Specific to Each Option

- **Scattered-site apartments:**
  Noisy clients;
  Bothersome friends or family members;
  Harboring runaways or other minors;
  Poor hygiene skills;
  Occasional damages;
  Moving evicted clients;
  Client loneliness.

- **Shared homes:**
  Problems due to mix of clients;
  Burnout of live-in staff;
  Arguments over food theft, telephone and TV use;
  Blaming other residents for problems;
  Breaking rules when resident manager is gone;
  Calls from neighbors about group gatherings.

- **Host homes:**
  Mismatch of youth and host lifestyles;
  Theft of host possessions;
  Uncertainty about where clients go at discharge.

- **Boarding home:**
  Clients dislike environment and lack of privacy;
  Fights between IL clients and aggressive residents;
  Clients must interview well to be accepted.

- **Roommate situations:**
  Theft of food and clothing and others' belongings;
  Arguments about visitors, music, use of phones, chores;
  Blaming roommates for problems, damages, and messes.

Liability/Risk Management Issues

The program tries to screen out highly irresponsible youth and removes a youth quickly if things get out of control. Landlords and resident managers are given contact information to reach staff and a copy of the program rules. Clients are moved into agency shelters, group homes, or foster homes if they prove unable to follow rules. Youth may be given another chance by being moved into another apartment or living arrangement. Referring agencies and the juvenile court are contacted to clear any needed placement change.

Weekly face-to-face meetings and apartment checks are expected of staff members, as is ongoing documentation of visits and phone contacts. Staff increase contact with youth having problems and will make numerous random visits. Youth with developmental disabilities are sometimes assigned "life coaches" who meet with them daily.

The agency carries insurance against major problems and pays cash for any damages. Clients are expected to reimburse the agency for any damages. Clients are informed that they reside in program leased or owned property and can be removed instantly if necessary.

Who Signs the Lease and Why?

The lease is signed in the agency's name with the youth as a co-signer. We do this to maintain control of the apartment if a placed youth doesn't work out in a particular apartment. If a youth has a job and has proven to be a responsible tenant, he/she can keep the apartment and all furnishings and have the lease and security deposit put in his/her name at discharge. About a third of our clients are in a position to do this.

After-Hours Crises

We have a rotating on-call schedule to handle crises. Staff average 2-3 calls a week after hours, with most "crises" able to be handled by phone in a few minutes. New clients often page the on-call person just to see if anyone really is out there.

What Seems to be Working in the Lighthouse ILP

Lighthouse and the local service community are encouraged by the results of using the scattered-site apartment model. The ILP is able to easily find landlords willing to rent to clients, and the geographical flexibility is appreciated by clients, referring agency caseworkers, and former foster parents. The ability to move youth who do not act responsibly from apartments back to agency-run shelters, group homes, and foster homes allows the program to give clients second chances and to keep landlords happy.

How Success is Measured

We look at the following six areas of client progress:

1. Youth leaves the program with an affordable and potentially long-term place to stay.

Over the years about 75% of our clients have left the program with a potentially long-term housing situation in place, whether it's the apartment we found for them or another situation they have chosen.

2. Youth gained significant employment experience or vocational training.

Around 60% of our youth gain employment experience. Teen moms might be discouraged from holding a job, as will students in challenging academic settings with a chance of getting a scholarship. Some youth in rural areas still in high school might not be able to get to and from a job while on their own.

3. Youth made progress toward educational goals.

This is usually a weak spot in our program. However, last year we had over 25 clients graduate from high school or receive their GED, a program record. Often, referred youth are so far behind in school that there is little chance of graduation while in county custody. These youth usually take GED classes and focus on

Staff Comment

"Nicole was terminated from our program for continuous rules infractions and was evicted from the apartment we found for her. She said she didn't care, she would move in with friends. Four years later she showed up at our office with a new hair color, a husband, a child, and a great job. She wanted to see if we remembered her (we did!) and asked me what she was like back in those days. She said she has very little memory of her days in ILP but started remembering her life skills lessons after finding herself without a place to stay."

finding employment. Some of our youth do not have the cognitive ability to pass a GED test, and we encourage them to find a full-time job.

4. Youth's awareness of family strengths and limitations has increased.

This is very hard to measure but is considered an important indicator of maturity and reality-based thinking. Youth who know how to connect to their families or understand the limits of family support fare better than those who cling to fantasies about reunification.

5. Youth's knowledge of independent living information has increased.

Youth are given a two-part information test at entry and discharge. Unfortunately, many youth are more motivated when taking the pretest, to prove they should be accepted into the program, than when taking the posttest, as they no longer feel they need to prove anything to ILP staff. We are working on a more valid way to assess their knowledge at discharge.

6. Youth's overall level of responsibility has increased.

This is measured at entry and termination using a simple scale created by program staff. Again, a flaw in this measure is that there are some youth who deliberately sabotage their life situation in order to buy more time in the system. They drop out of school with one quarter left or quit a job they had when entering the program. Most clients, however, really make progress toward taking charge of their lives.

Our Top Ten Most Common Problems with Clients

1. Youth who cannot control noisy, rowdy friends in their apartments.

2. Youth who are "hygienically challenged."

3. Youth who sabotage everything staff does for them.

4. Youth who don't appreciate the opportunities being offered.

5. Youth who actively avoid staff and miss appointments.

6. Damages caused by clients or friends.

7. Clients with long-term mental health issues who have difficulty following through on tasks.

8. Lost keys!!

9. Clients who see staff as adversaries.

10. Youth with anti-social tendencies who cannot follow anyone's rules.

Things Staff Would Like to See Happen

■ Extend lengths of supported time in the program, especially for youth with developmental disabilities or other significant long-term problems.

■ Terminate resistant youth and re-accept them when they are ready to go to work.

■ Halt the continuous growth of and changes in paperwork requirements.

■ Involve the rest of the system in the self-sufficiency preparation process.

■ Hire more people to work one-on-one with difficult clients.

■ Establish a fund for former clients who run into emergencies.

■ Obtain cars for youth who live in rural areas.

Most Common Staff-Related Problems

1. Communication about daily activities; especially, uncertainty about responsibilities.

2. Forgetting to cancel appointments when calling in sick.

3. Logistical issues and details around client moves.

4. Continuously changing and growing paperwork requirements.

5. When staff members avoid resistant, difficult, or needy clients.

6. When staff members assume that someone else will cover for their mistakes or forgetfulness.

7. "I know I was on call, but the battery must have died! I'm sorry you had to take that 2 a.m. page."

8. Caseload "meltdown" — when one person has too many "red flag" clients assigned to him/her.

How Lighthouse Deals with Client Evictions

Needless to say, placing teens in their own apartments is not without a lot of headaches. Our youth do what all of us did when we were teens, plus some other things. Over the course of a year, we always have 8-10 youth who are asked by their landlords to leave their apartments, usually due to excessive noise and visitors. We make it clear up front with landlords that we don't know how any of our new clients will react to their new-found freedom. We ask the landlords to give us some notice before a youth must leave, but if things are out of control, we have been known to arrive at an apartment with our van and numerous staff members ready to pack up a client's belongings and move him or her to a new location.

We utilize our "housing continuum" when this situation arises, moving a youth to our agency's crisis shelter, one of our group homes, another vacant apartment, a local boarding home, or one of our two shared homes. Being able to do this has enabled us to avoid bigger problems, such as lawsuits or extensive property damage. Landlords appreciate the speed at which we address client problems and often allow us to move another youth into an apartment recently vacated by a rowdy program participant.

We have moved some clients up to 4-5 times to find the best fit or bail them out of the consequences of their unruly behavior. You need a truck or van and a few available unemployed clients with strong backs to be able to respond to necessary "crisis moves." Most of our youth learn from the process of being evicted. Youth who grow up in group homes or residential treatment centers often look at a resident manager or landlord as just another caseworker or social worker. It takes them awhile to understand that landlords are really interested in just two things from them: their rent money and no problems.

7
Kenosha Independent Living Program

Kenosha, Wisconsin

Byron Wright

Brief History

The Kenosha Independent Living Program (ILP) was started in 1985 through an Innovative Youth Aids Grant awarded to Kenosha County by the State of Wisconsin. The original intent of the program was to start an eight-bed group home for older youth and have them earn vocational degrees. However, there was not enough money to run a group home, so Kenosha County contracted with Kenosha Youth Development Services (now Kenosha Human Development Services) to set up a different program.

Kenosha Human Development Services (herein referred to as KHDS) is a private, not-for-profit, social services agency that provides a variety of community programs on a contract basis with Kenosha County Human Services. KHDS set up a program that started out with a variety of scattered-site living arrangements and a four-bed group foster home. Over the years, the program has evolved to include two group homes, scattered-site living arrangements with case management and skill teaching, and after-care planning for all Kenosha County youth over 16 years old in alternative care.   KHDS also provides *transitional housing* for homeless youth and adult correctional clients with an additional 40 scattered-site and 17 residential beds in two community-based residential facilities.

KHDS is part of an integrated system of social services in Kenosha County. We provide 24-hour phone and face-to-face crisis counseling for adults and juveniles, while also gatekeeping the adult social service system for the mentally ill, developmentally disabled, and substance abusers. The provision of these and other adult services greatly enhances our ability to provide aftercare. The program description that follows deals with our scattered-site program for systems youth.

Description of the Program

The KHDS Independent Living Program (ILP) uses a scattered-site housing model. Our observation is that this approach provides greater flexibility for a variety of youth, is experiential in nature, is economical, and allows for tailoring living arrangements to fit the needs of individual youth. Our program also has a group center located in a downtown storefront that is used for offices, a classroom, storage of furniture and "starter kits," and as a place for the youth to visit. Almost all our youth live in individual living arrangements, as we have had little success with youth having roommates. The agency also has two group homes for older adolescents, but they are in a different agency division.

The program has a policy of accepting all Kenosha County referrals. This means that many of the youth we take are with us not because they are ready to live on their own but because there are simply no other available options. Many of the youth do not do well in group homes and are too old to become attached to foster parents. The youth come to the program with many issues, not the least of which are normal adolescent developmental challenges. We tailor each youth's program to fit his or her individual needs. This might mean making a change in the youth's living arrangement.

Staff Comment

> "It is our observation that most youth like the Independent Living Program. We know this, because they initiate a lot of contact with the staff and spend lots of time with the staff that is not required. We also have numerous youth who stay in touch with program staff for years after their participation in the program has ended. The former participants show up when they are doing well and also when they need help."

Outline of Program Services

Housing. Youth are placed in a variety of housing options including apartments, single room occupancy (SRO), and host homes. All youth receive help obtaining furnishings and are given basic household supplies. Most of our living arrangements do not require leases but are on a month-to-month basis. The SROs we use are on a weekly basis. The majority of our youth, with the exception of teen mothers with children, start in SROs. We find this to be most realistic, since many of our youth do not have the skills necessary to maintain an apartment when they initially enter the program.

Financial Support. The agency covers rent up to $300/month, and clients may earn a weekly allowance of $50 to $85, depending on their program level and how well they are doing. The weekly money is earned by the youth through a time-sheet approach that attaches a dollar amount to specific tasks. The youth and caseworker agree on the required time-sheet items, and each has a copy. We save 20% of what youths earn in an agency savings account and give it to them when they leave care, minus any outstanding bills. For those youth who are completely uninvested and earning no money, we have an arrangement with Franks Diner, a local

eatery, where youth get a $5 daily voucher for a meal. Franks is a unique place with regular employees who share a lot of care and concern for our youth. The three main employees have all been there over 10 years and know the nature of our program's clients.

Life Skills Training. All youth are taught tangible skills through an experiential approach and use the workbook, *Making It On Your Own*, by Dorothy Ansell (published by the National Resource Center for Youth Services). Intangible skill teaching relies on our agency experience with the *Teaching Family Model* (published by the Teaching Family Association) and a well developed, agency-designed social skills curriculum. Our staff approach in teaching skills is to be positive, nurturing, and encouraging, so youth are more receptive to skill teaching. Youth who are successfully involved in school or work need the least skills teaching, because they already are practicing many of the skills we teach.

Emotional Support/Guidance.   Each youth has a caseworker with an average case load of 9 to 13 youth. Our youth meet on a regular basis with their caseworker, and many often drop by the center unannounced. We also visit each youth at his or her living arrangement on a weekly basis. Our agency has a 24-hour phone and mobile crisis counseling service available to all youth. Some youth also regularly see therapists or psychologists. In addition, we encourage and facilitate contact with supportive family members and other adults who may develop into long-term networks of support.

Staff Comment

"Over the years, we have had clients come back to us after being gone three, four, five, and six years, to ask for help, or to tell us where their lives are going.
Sometimes the bonds created between staff and clients on Independent Living survive years later."

Case Management/Planning.   Every case plan is individual to a particular youth, and the youth directs the plan. The goal plans are written, and the long-range plans dictate the daily activities of the youth. Each plan is different, reflecting the unique set of skills and issues that each youth brings to the program. We realize that becoming a successful adult is a process, and it will not be completed in the short time we have with each program participant.

When youth leave, they are encouraged to stay in contact by an "open door" policy at the Independent Living Center. On average, we have 25-35 former clients stop in each month with specific issues or just to check in. We work with some former youth directly and also refer them to other community services.

Outreach.   The program is constantly involved in collaboration with other social service agencies, private employers, and landlords to insure that we have the resources necessary to help each youth meet his or her goals. We provide regular foster parent training and help every youth over 16 in care in Kenosha develop a plan for what happens when s/he ages out of the system. We are also involved in a statewide Independent Living Coalition and network nationally with other providers of similar services. We have helped three other Wisconsin counties develop scattered-site apartment programs.

Objective of Program

Our program objective is to prepare older adolescents to live independently as adults. To accomplish this we provide safe, secure living arrangements, case management, and skill teaching with an emphasis on individualized case planning. We realize that successful community living as an adult is a process not normally completed by program end. Therefore, it is essential that we have aftercare plans that continue to help youth in this process. Many of these plans include continued social services involvement from the adult side of services.

Average Daily Population

Our average daily population is about 110 youth. Those youth are served in the following categories:

Service Area	Number of Youth/Adults
Adult Case Management (ongoing case management for former program youth, funded by county adult social services)	10
Scattered-Site Living Arrangements (including case management, subsidized room and board, and skill teaching)	25
Transitional Living Group Home (youth 15½-17 years old who need group care for 6 months to a year)	5
Independent Living Group Home (short-term group care for youth who will transition to scattered sites)	7
Adult Living Skills	63

Geographical Range — Areas Served

The majority of our youth are from Kenosha County, with about 10% of placements from surrounding counties. The program sees for discharge planning all youth over 16 years old placed in alternate care by Kenosha County, regardless of where they are located. Many youth are in group homes or treatment foster homes located outside Kenosha County.

Funding Sources

Most program funds are provided by Kenosha County. We also charge a daily rate of $29.60 for youth placed from other counties and a contact rate of $25.48 each time we see them, with a maximum of one charged contact per day. We also receive Kenosha County's share of the Federal

Independent Living Initiative dollars and get some grant money through the State Division of Housing.

Assessment of Client Strengths and Needs

We assess client strengths and needs through the following methods:

- Strengths Needs Assessment

- Referral information that includes a social history, psychological evaluations, and school records

- Observation of youth

- Interviews with social workers and significant others in the youth's life

- Agency peer review with the staff psychiatrist and psychologist

Life Skills Training Strategies

The program teaches life skills through a combination of classes and an experiential approach. Twice weekly we have skills classes that focus on tangible or intangible skills. We use the workbook, *Making It On Your Own*, as a guide for teaching tangible skills in the classroom. However, much of our skills teaching takes place on a daily basis with individual clients. We have found that actual experience is preferable to classroom experience.

For example, if the skill is obtaining employment, we first have the youth fill out a mock application, practice interviewing, teach them how to look for jobs in the newspaper, and then actually take them out to get applications. Next we have them check over the application, practice an interview for a specific job, and take them to the interview. Following that we process with the youth how the interview went, go over with them employer expectations for job performance, and help them problem solve as issues arise on the job. Our philosophy is that experiential teaching is most effective.

When it comes to teaching intangible skills, we rely on our agency experience with the *Teaching Family Model* (*TFM*). This model has a well defined set of social skills that we teach youth and encourage them to use.

Staff Comment

"There is a constant communication between the clients and staff to determine how the program functions as a whole. Some of our best policy changes have come as a result of a client's idea. And this is one of the reasons this program works, through its fluidity and sensitivity to the needs of the kids over time."

Having appropriate social skills is the key to negotiating the everyday encounters in a successful adult's life. Many of our youth have skills for dealing with people that work well "on the streets" but do not work very well on the job, with landlords, or in school. We give them a new set of skills to use.

Our approach with youth is positive and encouraging, to help them build appropriate relationships. Many youth are from emotionally chaotic situations, so we are calm, nurturing, and supportive. When youth feel better about themselves, they are much more likely to be able to get on with the task of becoming successful adults.

> **Staff Comment**
>
> "Normally, our biggest complaint from youth is that they are lonely, and all want to live in their own apartments immediately. They also express some concerns, because they view us as having too high expectations for them being on time and leading a structured, well-ordered life."

Client Involvement in Program Development

All youth are involved in designing their own particular program to meet their goals. Each youth has the greatest say in what his or her goals are while in the program and what tasks need to be accomplished to meet those goals. Youth also teach classes, prepare meals for classes, and on a regular basis make suggestions about what program changes would be helpful. Running a scattered-site program means that, by design, youth have to be in control of their particular plan and their life in general.

Types of Housing Options Utilized by the Kenosha ILP

Description, Cost, Advantages, and Disadvantages of Current Housing Options

Our program relies on an array of housing options that range from SROs to apartments. We also have youth who live with non-program roommates and are in host homes. We see that having an array of placements best suits the diversity of youth we serve. Because of our "no reject" referral policy, we accept a number of youth who are simply not mature enough for apartment living. The following is a description of our housing options, along with the cost, advantages, and disadvantages of each.

Single Room Occupancy - ($300/month)

We rely mainly on the Kenosha Youth Foundation (KYF), which is Kenosha's equivalent of the YWCA. It has full recreational facilities and 99 furnished single rooms. All of our youth have full use of the facilities, which include three gyms, a weight room, and two pools. We have staff on the rooming floors on second and third shift in a program for homeless adults funded through a HUD grant. We also use the Plaza Hotel. This is a downtown rooming house with 25 rooms and an on-site manager. We use two other local SROs on an infrequent basis.

Advantages of SROs:

- Less isolation than an apartment.
- On-site supervision.
- Use of the recreational facilities at KYF.
- Can accept youth who aren't mature enough to live in an apartment.
- Will give any ILP client a chance to live there (easy in, easy out resource).
- Close to staff (ILP center is two blocks from KYF and the Plaza).

Disadvantages of SROs:

- Lack of privacy.
- Youth living there can spend too much time together.
- Problems with other long-term SRO residents.
- No "commons" area for visiting with friends.

Host Homes - ($300/month for room and board)

Host homes are always found by the youth who want to live with host adult(s). Many times hosts are parents of a school friend, a former neighbor, or occasionally a former foster home. We investigate the living arrangement and decide if it is appropriate for the youth. We also determine if it is safe for the person providing the arrangement, since sometimes people make fairly uninformed decisions about letting a somewhat chaotic 17-year-old live in their home. It is important that the house have clear expectations for a youth's behavior prior to the start of the living arrangement.

Staff Comment

"If there is one thing we have heard most often from returning clients, it is that they wish they had done more, and taken even more advantage of the services offered, while they were here."

Advantages of Host Homes:

- Family environment.
- Positive role modeling.
- Less isolation.

- More support than living on your own.
- Greater structure.
- Good homes are like "24-hour staff."

Disadvantages of Host Homes:

- Youth may have problems dealing with family dynamics.
- Unrealistic expectations of host home for teenage behavior.
- Youth or family may take advantage of one another.

Apartments - ($300-$425/month)

We have a network of landlords who rent to us on a regular basis with a variety of efficiency, one-bedroom, and two-bedroom apartments. We pay all landlords the rent directly and will move the youth on short notice if there are problems. We will also clean up the apartment if necessary. Our relationship with landlords is so positive that many call us first if they have a vacant apartment.

> **Staff Comment**
>
> "As a rule, we do not have our youth share living arrangements. We tried 15 or 20 roommate situations, and our success rate was zero. They either did not get along, had twice the 'traffic' of one person, or one's financial disaster would mean that half the rent wasn't paid, and both would lose a place to live."

Advantages of Apartments:

- More privacy.
- Youth can take over living arrangement after program ends.
- Most realistic living arrangement to prepare youth to live on their own.
- More comfortable than SROs.

Disadvantages of Apartments:

- Problems with neighbors and landlords due to noise and traffic.
- Can be isolating for youth.
- Greater expense with utilities.
- Demand on staff time in helping move clients and furnishing apartments.
- May have other non-program people (particularly family) move in with them.

Liability/Risk Management Issues

Liability issues have not arisen in the 14 years we have run the program. The most effective risk management tools are regular apartment visits, close landlord relationships, and clear statements of what is expected in a particular living arrangement. We also encourage landlords to let us know immediately if there are problems, rather than letting problems build up. The agency carries liability insurance covering all employees.

Who Signs the Lease and Why?

Most of our living arrangements do not require leases. Apartments are on a month-to-month basis and the SROs on a weekly basis. If a lease is signed, it is by the youth. The protection we offer landlords is through monitoring the youth, paying the rent directly, and a willingness to move youth on short notice. If damages occur, we negotiate some reimbursement with the landlord and require the youth to pay, with money from either their savings or their weekly earnings.

What Seems to be Working in the KHDS Program

Staff Comment

"We have clients who have lost two, three, maybe even more places to live during their time here, but everything is a learning process, both the mistakes and the successes."

The KHDS program is committed to the individual scattered-site living approach. We are also firmly convinced that individual goal plans that accept youth at their particular developmental level are much more effective than making the youth "fit the program." We keep working with youth regardless of the difficulty they present, so, although there may be failed living arrangements, youth may not fail out of the program. We are also firmly committed to an experiential approach in teaching tangible skills and are very invested in teaching social skills.

How Success is Measured

We have no formal measures of success in our program. However, for many years Kenosha County surveyed our delinquent youth for new criminal behavior while in the program and 6 months post discharge. Our youth had the highest risk factor ratings and one of the lowest levels of re-offense. Over a 5-year period, our average rate of recidivism was only around 20%!

All youth have goal plans, and the majority make some progress toward their goals. The following are staff estimates of the percentage of clients that make progress toward particular goal areas:

Goal	Percentage
▪ Housing when youth leave the program	80%
▪ Employment experience	60%
▪ Educational goals	33% graduate from high school or obtain GEDs

We are planning to start measuring progress toward these goals in the upcoming year.

Our Top Ten Most Common Problems

1. Youth maintaining living arrangements.

2. Too little time with youth with marginal skills entering the program.

3. Not enough positive adult support for the youth from outside the program, particularly from family.

4. Tight budgetary constraints that interfere with our ability to provide all the services we would like.

5. The most dysfunctional youth forming negative relationships with one another.

6. The hassles of moving youth and getting them to understand how to prepare for a move.

7. Providing enough structure and support for teen mothers with small children.

8. Managing the center when many youth are "hanging out."

9. Transportation, since our city bus service runs only until 6 p.m., and many youth have trouble

Staff Comment

"We have developed an ongoing case management service for some clients that allows us to continue to work with them as adults. This service, funded by Kenosha County, has enabled us to keep some of our clients for as long as seven years. The ability to provide this ongoing case management has greatly enhanced quality of life for some of our most needy clients. The clients we keep normally have a combination of developmental disabilities and little or no family support."

obtaining driver's licenses and automobiles.

10. Keeping tabs on potential criminal behavior when we have a large number of delinquent youth.

Things Staff Would Like to See Happen

Staff Comment

"One client, who made her share of mistakes on our program, came back simply to say thanks, and to tell us of the family she now has and house she now resides in. On this program, the staff doesn't give up on the kids, and the benefits to these clients, though they may not be seen immediately, can be seen months and years later, when they remember the things that they were taught and the examples they learned from."

■ A full-time staff person for five teen mothers with children.

■ More time to spend with the least functional youth.

■ The funds necessary to hire someone to move youth.

■ Mentors for all youth who need and want them.

■ A kitchen at our center to teach cooking skills.

■ A more efficient system of paperwork, with fewer competing requirements from different funding sources.

■ An increase in program length up to age 21 for many youth.

■ Ways for youth to get driver's licenses and vehicles while in the program.

■ Ways to measure outcomes that are simple and objective.

■ Development of a more structured setting for respite for youth who are floundering.

Most Common Staff-Related Problems

1. Getting paperwork turned in on a timely basis.

2. Coordinating client moves.

3. Different staff staying consistent with clients who have similar issues. (Particularly with those youth whose persistence can wear you down.)

4. Keeping the center clean and organized.

5. Keeping appointments on time.

6. Walking the "fine line" between enabling and expecting too much from youth.

How Kenosha ILP Deals with Client Drug and Alcohol Use

We encourage our youth to refrain from the use of drugs and alcohol. Such use is not only illegal, it also many times interferes with their ability to achieve the goals of maintaining housing and employment and succeeding in school. However, we fully expect that many of our youth will use, and we normally continue to work with them. We do not spend a lot of time trying to figure out which youth have substance abuse problems, since their behavior while using brings them to our attention.

Our main program strategies for dealing with substance use are:

1. Teach classes on the effects of drug and alcohol use. We also focus on the impact of use on families, since many of our youth grew up in families with these issues.

2. Youth with substance abuse problems come to our attention, because use causes them to lose jobs, miss school, be kicked out of their living arrangement, and have police contact. These real-life consequences are immediate, may be harsh, and can be a learning experience that encourages youth to change their behavior.

3. Many of our youth are from homes that were abusive and traumatic, and they use drugs or alcohol to "self medicate." AODA masks a lot of pain. We work to involve youth in counseling to deal with those issues instead of masking the pain with substance abuse.

In our culture today, many youth experiment with drugs and alcohol. Alcohol use has long been a cultural norm here. There are 156 taverns in our town of 80,000. It would be unrealistic to expect complete abstinence from our youth. Our best hope is to give them plenty of education about substance abuse and teach to the consequences that oft-times occur when they are using.

8

Quakerdale Independent Living Program

New Providence, Iowa

Cheryl Tanis

Brief History

Quakerdale is one of Iowa's largest private, non-profit child welfare agencies. Quakerdale was founded in 1851 by Josiah White, a Philadelphia Quaker who left funds through his estate to establish an orphanage. Today, Quakerdale is a multi-service child welfare agency. Along with Cluster-Site and Scattered-Site Independent Living Services, Quakerdale provides Family Centered Services, Family Foster Care and Adoption Services, Adolescent Day Treatment, Residential Treatment, School-Based Support Services, After-School Services, and Shelter Care. Quakerdale provides services on four campuses located in Waterloo, Marshalltown, Manning, and New Providence. The agency serves clients from all over Iowa. Referrals primarily come from The Department of Human Services or Juvenile Court Services. Clients are usually adjudicated Child In Need of Assistance or Delinquent.

In 1992, our residential treatment population decreased due to placement practices in Iowa. With so many foster children aging out of the system, it became apparent that Quakerdale needed to add to its array of services by including independent living programming.

In July 1993, Quakerdale entered into a purchase of service contract with the State of Iowa to provide Cluster-Site and Scattered-Site Independent Living Services. The Independent Living Services are fully funded through our purchase of service contract with the State.

Both programs were initiated on the New Providence Campus and were later expanded to include Scattered-Site services on the other campuses. Currently Quakerdale's New Providence campus is the only Cluster-Site Independent Living program in Iowa.

Description of the Program

Client Comments

"I like being able to go to concerts, go out to eat, and to go on home visits."

"I don't like staff pressure about our friends."

"I like the staff helping me learn to live on my own."

Independent Living Services are designed to help adolescents' transition from residential treatment and/or family foster care to independent living and eventually emancipation. Cluster-Site Services provide supervised apartment living with 24-hour staff supervision. The Scattered-Site Independent Living Service provides approximately 20 hours per month of staff monitoring and support for clients who reside in their own rented community housing.

Participants in the program are adolescents 16 to 19 years old who are completing their high school or high school equivalency (GED) diplomas or are in a college program. Clients under age 18 must be working, in work training full-time, or completing high school while working part-time. Clients age 18 or older must be attending school or working on a GED full-time and making satisfactory progress toward completion of high school or a GED program.

Quakerdale Independent Living Program Objectives

The primary goal of the Independent Living Service is to help youth meet their basic needs and build competencies in preparation for self-sufficiency. In order to achieve that programmatic goal, the staff attends to the following objectives:

1. Assessing each youth's life skills development needs, based on the Daniel Memorial Independent Living Assessment for Life Skills.

2. Identifying and developing individual strengths, coping skills, social

skills, and life management skills.

3. Identifying academic and career goals and developing school skills.

4. Teaching skills, such as budgeting and money management, cooking, general behaviors, consumer skills, interpersonal relationships and communication (building and maintaining relationships), social skills, personal care, household management, and community resource utilization and support system development, to assist youth in becoming self-sufficient.

5. Providing opportunity for career development, which includes career exploration, vocational skills training, and job seeking and keeping skill development.

6. Promoting school attendance and academic achievement, such as high school completion, vocational-technical skills training, and/or post-secondary education.

7. Teaching the Three R's of Responsibility, which are reliability, respectfulness, and resourcefulness.

Client Comment

"I don't like the arguing and people putting others down." (This was a comment about the community living arrangement.)

8. Providing, to the degree possible, a fail-safe learning environment in which youth can make mistakes, recover from these mistakes, and use them as an opportunity to learn different strategies for successful life management.

How Success is Measured

Success in the program is measured through the youth's ability to:

■ Demonstrate self-sufficiency;

■ Utilize community resources, such as substance abuse support services, churches, mentors, job training opportunities, mental health services, medical services, and legal services;

■ Remain free from illegal entanglements and risky behaviors;

■ Find and maintain housing;

■ Secure positive peer relationships;

■ Demonstrate responsible sexual and social behavior;

- Find and keep employment; and

- Attain career and educational training and goals, e.g., high school completion, job training, and post-secondary education.

Average Daily Population

The average population in the Cluster-Site Independent Living program is six, and the average in the Scattered-Site Independent Living program is five. However, we have had as many as ten clients in the Scattered-Site program.

Staffing

Both Cluster-Site and Scattered-Site programs receive overall supervision from the campus director, who serves as the clinical supervisor to the caseworker. The caseworker is the team leader for the independent living staff. The staff includes two full-time direct care staff and one part-time support staff. The management of the two programs is a team effort, with staff members having primary responsibility for the areas described below.

The specific duties of the caseworker include the following: program and case management; intake and discharge processing; case work treatment planning and documentation, which includes assessments and progress reports; individual and group counseling and skill development; crisis management; family, referring worker, community, school, and employer collaboration and networking.

The direct care staff is primarily responsible for the Cluster-Site Independent Living residents. However, they provide back-up support and services to the Scattered-Site youth. Their duties include the following: on-site, 24-hour-a-day supervision of the residents; insuring safety and security of the youth; transportation; school and employer liaison; skill instruction; counseling; crisis management; cottage management; oversight for youth with activities of daily living, such as money management, grocery shopping, homework, social skills, and behavior management.

> ### Client Comment
>
> *"I don't like the lack of staff."* (We have a ratio of 1 staff to 6 youth, with an additional staff person scheduled for times when there are more activities planned and heavy transportation needs.)

Assessment of Client Strengths and Needs

The State of Iowa has transitional living specialists, who provide a Daniel Memorial Independent Living Assessment for Life Skills (DMLS) for all youth who are in the system during their 16th year. The Quakerdale caseworker does the assessment for those youth who have not received one. In addition, we chart daily session notes on each youth in Cluster-Site and each session with Scattered-Site youth. Staff observation and ongoing dialogue with the residents help the staff in the assessment of each youth's personal strengths, needs, feelings, and hopes for the future. The DMLS assessment areas are the key measures by which the youth's progress in gaining life skills is measured. The initial DMLS assessment is used as a baseline to measure progress toward self-sufficiency.

Life Skills Training Strategies

Staff utilizes several strategies to teach life skills. Approaches include the use of mentors from the school, church, job sites, and concerned citizens; group and individual counseling; life skills training curriculum packets; and the utilization of immediate ongoing feedback, support, and teaching.

Mentors provide skills training and personal support to the Independent Living clients. Teachers, coaches, ministers, church youth groups, several local employers, and Fun Families (local volunteer support families or individuals) mentor the youth. In addition, landlords who are flexible and willing to work with youth learning how to manage the responsibilities of renting are utilized.

Group and individual counseling services are built into the Independent Living Service. Eight hours of group counseling per month are provided to the youth. Individual counseling services include 8 hours per week for the Cluster-Site youth and 5 hours per week for the Scattered-Site youth. The staff uses group and individual time to teach, role model, practice, and encourage youth to learn, practice, and integrate their life skill education in their daily lives. These group and individual sessions are an excellent opportunity to teach life skills and practice effective decision making, interpersonal communication, and problem-solving skills. The sessions are also designed to address the Three R's of Responsibility, as noted above. The group setting also allows peers an opportunity to teach each other, using the lessons they have learned from their own life experience.

Client Comments

"I like buying my own food and having my own room."

"I feel good about having a job."

"I like getting to structure my own time."

Life Skills packets with the content areas listed below are utilized to insure consistency in skills training for all youth. Use of the curriculum in these packets, coupled with real-life hands-on practice of such life skills as shopping and consumer skills, job training and career exploration, service learning, and apartment hunting, is the core skills development strategy.

- Introduction to Independent Living: Social Security number, birth certificate, vital statistics, family history, finding personal belongings, etc.
- Budgeting
- Clothing
- Food and Nutrition
- Banking
- Health Care
- Leisure Time Activities and Recreation
- Personal Records and Information
- Employment
- Child Care
- Community Resources
- Education
- Self-Understanding, Coping Skills, and Self-Esteem
- Transportation
- Housing
- Furnishings
- Buying a Car
- Final Project

Client Involvement in Program Development

Program development is ultimately governed at the board or advisory board level. The board members are appointees from the Iowa Yearly Friends, the regional Quaker Church governing body. Some board-appointed advisory committees exist, such as the program committee, and parents of clients have been invited to participate. Currently youth are not included in these committees. However, the program committee has sought youth input, through a formal interviewing process, when it has conducted in-depth program reviews.

On Sunday nights a community group meeting is conducted. All of the youth in the program are invited to this meeting. The community meeting provides an opportunity for youth to give input into the program design, share concerns, and solve program management problems. In addition, individuals are

Client Comments

"I don't like living out in the country." (The program is located 10 miles from the nearest town.)

"I like being able to play sports."

"I like being able to go to school."

free to give input to the staff on program management and development at any time.

Types of Housing Options Utilized by the Quakerdale Program

The Cluster-Site Independent Living program is located on campus. A maximum of six residents can be housed in individual apartments, which are similar to dormitory rooms. The residents share common living room, dining room, recreation, laundry room, and kitchen areas. Currently, residents in the Cluster-Site program are limited to 6 months in the program. At 6 months they are discharged into the Scattered-Site program or are emancipated. Iowa's Administrative Rules are being changed to allow for placements that are longer than 6 months. However, official notification has not yet been received about this change.

Scattered-Site apartments are located both on campus and in the towns surrounding Quakerdale. Two on-campus apartments are available, one for girls and one for boys, which hold up to three residents each. In essence, these on-site apartments create a unique step-down Independent Living program option.

The on-site apartments are located in two cottages. One cottage houses the Cluster-Site program and the other a Residential Treatment program. These on-campus apartments allow for oversight with youth who are not quite ready to manage on their own. This option also allows youth who have not gained sufficient confidence, responsibility, financial security, community resources, and life management skills to live totally separate from the campus.

The disadvantage of this program is that it can create concerns about residents who may become too dependent. This occurs primarily with residents who are struggling socially, developmentally, and academically. However, the additional support and supervision that this step-down option provides have enhanced the chances for successful outcomes for many of the residents in their quest for self-sufficiency.

In addition to the on-campus facilities, apartments in surrounding towns are used for independent living. Usually the youth cannot afford to live in very good housing. The staff assesses each apartment regarding safety, cleanliness, and security standards prior to a client moving into the apartment. Each youth must have a phone at his or her residence and is required to maintain a clean, safe, and secure residence. The apartments are checked minimally one time per week to insure that program standards are met.

Generally, housing costs range from $250 to $400 per month, plus a down payment of 1 month's rent and utility start-up fees. Gathering enough money to establish a home base away from the campus within 6 months has been difficult. The added stress of obtaining enough funds to secure transportation to get to school and work in rural Iowa impacts the youth's choices of housing. There is no mass transit in rural Iowa, so youth must purchase their own cars or arrange for transportation from others. Signing lease contracts has also been difficult. If the parent, legal guardian, or referring worker is not willing to sign the lease, then the cottage case-worker is left with that responsibility and the risks involved. Problems in renting off campus have occurred, with both clients and landlords not following through on their commitments, as well as with public relations concerns and youth engaging in risky and illegal activities.

What Seems to be Working in the Quakerdale ILP

Several components of the program have worked well, and they include the following:

■ The Life Skills Packet work gives youth concrete skills and knowledge they need to gain in preparation for self-sufficiency.

Client Comments

"I don't like staff wanting to know everything we say or do."

"I like having helpful staff and getting help when I need it."

■ The group and individual counseling sessions provide a useful forum for regularly engaging in formal face-to-face support and skill development sessions with the youth.

■ The on-campus Scattered-Site apartments provide an additional level of support that most independent living programs do not have.

■ Although the rural setting and small-town atmosphere have created problems regarding transportation, employment resources, and public relations, these characteristics also tend to keep the youth safer and less apt to get into serious legal problems.

■ Students have excellent educational resources, in that community colleges, alternative schools, and good public schools are available to them locally. Most of the teachers are genuinely helpful in supporting program participants' academic success. The youth are often on the honor roll and usually receive passing grades.

■ Strong community relationships exist with our youth, as evidenced by church and community members who seek them out to support, invest in, and mentor. In addition, the employers who provide job training and employment opportunities for the youth, as well as the school personnel and coaches who provide necessary encouragement, have demonstrated investment in and commitment to their growth.

■ The program structure has served the youth well, in that they are held accountable for their behavior and expected to be responsible.

■ Our youth have generally been successful at their places of employment and have usually found satisfactory employment opportunities.

■ Youth have access to staff. The caseworker's office is located in the cottage, which also adds necessary support to the direct care staff.

■ The State Training School for boys (9 miles away) and the State Juvenile Home (50 miles away) have used the Independent Living Services frequently.

■ The Independent Living Services provide an excellent transition program to boys and girls who do not have reliable family resources, no longer want to go to a foster home, and are no longer in need of residential treatment services.

Our Most Common Problems

The most common problems we have in providing these services include:

1. Finding adequate employment opportunities with reasonable hours for students is difficult in a small community.

2. Managing negative and sometimes untruthful stories about our Independent Living youth and their activities, as well as their very public mistakes, has been difficult in a community where news travels fast.

3. Quakerdale youth have difficulty being accepted by some of the teachers and students at school, which negatively impacts their search for social, employment, and academic success.

4. Many of the residents equate independent living with freedom from responsibility. As a result, we have youth whose attitudes, dishonesty, delinquent thinking, and lack of reliability hinder their success and the success of the program. A change in the name of the program could potentially help set the stage for more responsible participation in the program.

5. The low state reimbursement rate for services provided forces us to run

a very lean program. More staff, at least two on during prime-time hours and a full-time overnight-awake staff, would greatly relieve the staff's stress and increase program participants' freedom.

6. Transportation needs in the rural setting lead to a significant amount of time on the road. Since 100% supervision is required, all of the Cluster-Site youth must ride along on trips that are not made for them.

7. These youth have difficulty with fear, grief, and loss issues; their lack of adequate family resources, input, and support; and feeling connected to the larger community as they age out of the system.

8. Expanding services to include youth up to age 21 would greatly improve outcomes for youth who are lagging developmentally, who have difficulty learning the necessary skills for self-sufficiency, or for youth who have not chosen to act responsibly and need supervisory oversight to hold them accountable.

Client Viewpoints

Client Comment

"I don't like the slow transportation." (Youth often have to wait for the staff to come and pick them up.)

When past and present participants were asked what they liked and disliked about the program, they generally stated that they liked having the opportunity to be responsible for themselves. They also appreciated staff support in a comfortable home-like environment. Youth who have been discharged from the program and living on their own for several months stated that, while they were in the program, they felt the staff were often overbearing. However, now that they have been on their own, they value the staff support received and continue to call or stop by the cottage to visit with staff and/or to seek staff advice and support.

Service Rates

Youth in both the Scattered-Site and Cluster-Site programs receive a monthly stipend of $496.40 from the State of Iowa for basic living expenses. However, the stipend is not enough to help the youth be financially secure. They are expected to work at least part-time to earn enough money to help them cover their expenses and to meet the program expectation of developing employment skills.

The State of Iowa's Independent Living service reimbursement to Quakerdale is based on an hourly billable unit. The service rate is divided into the two program areas, Cluster-Site Independent Living and Scattered-Site Independent Living. Each of these services then is divided between group and individual services. The current service rates are as follows:

Cluster-Site:	Individual Services	$94.82 per hour
	Group Services	$34.38 per hour
Scattered-Site:	Individual Services	$45.21 per hour
	Group Services	$25.63 per hour

Generally, Quakerdale bills a range of 20 to 30 hours of individual services per month and 8 hours of group services per youth in the programs.

Summary

Overall, Quakerdale's Independent Living Services have provided a vital support system for youth who would otherwise be homeless or in less desirable living arrangements. Quakerdale has been very successful in the delivery of these services within Iowa. The feedback received from youth, their families, and the referring workers indicates that our services provide the quality and outcomes desired to help youth become self-sufficient and responsible adults.

Independent Living Staff Characteristics

When interviewing prospective Independent Living staff, we seek several individual characteristics and skills. Candidates must demonstrate that they:

• are respectful in their approach to working with youth;
• are focused on developing youth's strengths and assets;
• find ways to empower the youth as they develop self-management skills;
• have a firm and fair approach to guidance and discipline that helps youth learn from their mistakes;
• know how to provide youth with a sense of safety and security;
• are able to role model and teach conflict management effectively;
• can teach and role model effective problem solving and decision making;
• can act decisively, think on their feet, and manage crisis;
• demonstrate that they believe in the youth and their ability to be successful;
• have the patience to teach youth life management skills and pro-social values in a fail-safe environment;
• know how to build community networks and how to use community resources;
• understand the child welfare system and the effects of being a child of the system on the youth;
• can teach youth budgeting and consumer skills, time and leisure management, job seeking and keeping skills, interpersonal relationship skills, decision-making and problem-solving skills, school skills, household management skills, medical and self-care skills, etc.

In essence, their role is that of a mentor who acts as a guide to the youth as they learn their adult responsibilities. In addition, there are parenting skills that staff need. However, the parent role is best when democratic approaches to providing guidance and structure are in place and when autocratic or permissive approaches are avoided. The staff are primarily role models for the youth in the utilization of successful adult living skills, and they assist the youth in developing these same skills by creating a learning environment based on respect, positive communication, and support.

The staff hired for Independent Living differ from those in residential treatment programs, in that they tend to allow more room for errors and mistakes in the youth's judgement. They approach these mistakes as real-life opportunities to learn while the safety net of the program is still in place. In addition, they are more focused on helping youth develop life management skills than on therapeutic issues.

9
Open-Inn Independent Living Services

Tucson, Arizona

Trevor Atwood, Nancy Panico Lydic,
and Darlene G. Dankowski

Brief History

Open-Inn, Inc. was the first agency in Arizona to serve runaway and homeless youth. Based in Tucson (Pima County), Open-Inn has been working for 25 years to empower children, youth, and families to experience and develop positive self-worth. The cornerstone of the agency's services has been temporary and transitional shelter for homeless youth under age 18. Through a collaborative effort in 1987, Open-Inn began offering independent living services to private and systems youth through Life Skills Training, teaching at-risk young adults the practical skills necessary for self-sufficiency. In 1988, Open-Inn added housing and case management to its independent living services; the Transitional Apartment Living Program (TALP) was established in response to the growing need for a long-term placement for youth who could not, for one reason or another, return home. In 1994, Open-Inn expanded its independent living services through the CASA (Coalition Assisting Self-Sufficiency Attainment) program to include a scattered-site model apartment setting, providing housing for those youth ages 18-21 who no longer had the support of the system or a family. Beginning in 1997, Open-Inn expanded its Independent Living Services to three rural counties in Arizona. Drawing from our experience in Tucson, we have developed Life Skills Training, peer counseling, teen parent transitional shelter, and transitional living in a group setting for youth ages 16-18.

Open-Inn's intent is to develop the necessary continuum of care for homeless youth and to provide a full range of services directly or in conjunction with outside agencies. The project utilizes a simple, straightforward approach that opens doors for non-systems youth who would otherwise be denied access to a comprehensive continuum of care. When family reunification is not feasible or desirable, it is essential that youth be afforded the opportunity to gain new skills and competencies to support a gradual adjustment to independent living.

Description of the Program

Open-Inn's Independent Living Services seek to support and assist homeless young adults as they transition to independence. By providing outreach, housing, case management, and life skills education, Open-Inn creates opportunities for homeless youth to become responsible, self-sufficient adults. The programs emphasize commonsense decision making and future planning.

Outline of Open-Inn Services and Programs

Outreach. Community Outreach is conducted by two or three Peer Counselors, youth who have some experience with homelessness or near-homelessness. Along with an Outreach Specialist, Peer Counselors visit schools, neighborhood centers, and community locations where at-risk youth spend time or obtain services. Outreach consists of describing services available through Open-Inn, providing referral information for other services, and establishing initial contact with potential program participants. This project also subcontracts to provide individual and group sexual abuse counseling.

TALP. The Transitional Apartment Living Program serves male and female youth ages 16½ to 18. The agency offers on-site housing in a duplex of six two-bedroom apartments. A Houseparent lives on-site. Each youth works with a Case Manager to develop goals including education, employment, life skills training, and money management. Clients are referred by a variety of system and non-system sources, including self-referrals. The program is able to accommodate up to two small children of clients, allowing young single parents to participate in services.

CASA. The Coalition Assisting Self-Sufficiency Attainment program works with homeless young adults ages 18-21. Through CASA, Open-Inn has an average of ten scattered-site apartment slots for youth who wish to receive housing and case management as they further their education and save income. Clients are able to conduct an apartment search and select their apartment with the approval of a Case Manager. During the early phase of the program, clients can receive food vouchers, apartment furnishings and supplies, and utility assistance. Program participants receive life skills training from Open-Inn and job search training, as well as educational and vocational assessments, through the Jackson Employment Center, a local agency focusing on employment and training. Each client works with a Jackson Case Manager to formulate an Educational Development Plan and selects a vocational training or college program in his or her chosen career field. This education is fully subsidized through the program. If participants have not completed high school, they first earn their diploma through the agency charter school or participate in intensive GED remediation and obtain their GED. While attending school full-time, clients also work part-time and practice money management. Participants meet on a regular basis with their Case Manager to track their progress, budget finances, and discuss decisions. Case Management includes ongoing assessment and community referral for services as needed. The end goal for CASA clients is to utilize their education and training to obtain higher wage employment and assume their rent.

Staff Comment

"Felicia showed up at our company Christmas party last year. She was strung out on heroin and hungry. A fellow 'street kid' told her about us. We gave her some food and explained our housing programs but never expected to see her again. We were wrong. Over the next few weeks she came by on a regular basis to use the phone for job hunting, request batteries so she could read in her car at night (that was her 'home'), or to just 'hang out'. By February she had remained clean for 2 months and seemed ready to trust us, so we housed her in one of our units where she worked full time, fixed her car, and saved enough money to head back to Tennessee to live near her ailing grandma, which was her goal all along. She was probably one of the most grateful clients we've had — we were sad to see her go but glad we were able to help her."

Life Skills Program. This copyrighted program is designed to introduce youth between the ages of 15-21 to the skills necessary to transition into independence. All clients who participate in independent living housing services receive life skills training. Open-Inn also provides life skills training throughout Arizona as a required component of the Arizona Young Adult Program (AYAP) of the Administration for Children, Youth and Families (ACYF). The class meets three nights a week for 8 weeks. The program provides information in areas such as job readiness, housing, home management, health, education, consumerism, transportation, leisure activities, and value exploration. Students also receive resiliency training and practice money management through a finance project on a weekly basis. Volunteer guest speakers are utilized whenever possible and appropriate. Each youth is given a pre-assessment and a post-test. Students who successfully complete the program receive a Certificate of Completion.

Rural Programs. The Cochise County Children's Center (CCCC) is an emergency shelter licensed for 18 children, birth to age 17. The age range allows us to provide housing for up to two teen parents with child. In collaboration with other local agencies providing parenting support, the Center provides transitional housing for up to 90 days, case management, and Life Skills Training.

> **Staff Comment**
>
> *"I love my job, they're [homeless youth] so thankful for the smallest things — it makes us really feel good."*

At Crossroads Youth Services in Cottonwood and Turning Point in Prescott (both in Yavapai County), Open-Inn has expanded its shelter capacity to accommodate an increasing need for independent living. Services include transitional housing in a shelter setting, case management, Life Skills Training, peer counseling, and outreach.

The Alternatives Center for Family-Based Services in Flagstaff (Coconino County) provides Life Skills Training. Open-Inn is in the process of collaborating with Catholic Social Services to open a group home focused on independent living within the next 2 years in the area.

Open-Inn Program Objectives

The primary goal of these programs is to assist 16-21 year old homeless youth in transitioning successfully to self-sufficient living in order to prevent long-term dependency on social services, through the accomplishment of five major objectives:

1. Utilize an outreach component to identify homeless youth through a single point-of-entry.

2. Provide a stable and safe living environment in a supervised transitional setting and a scattered-site model while offering direct services and referrals to assist youth in preparing for a self-sufficient lifestyle.

3. Provide formalized Life Skills Training to equip the youth with the skills needed to sustain independence and positive lifestyles.

4. Provide opportunities to increase education level and employability skills.

5. Provide a safety net where youth can experience "real life" and natural consequences and learn from mistakes.

Average Daily Population

Pima County

TALP:	7 youth on an average daily basis
CASA:	8-12 youth on an average daily basis
Life Skills:	15 youth per class
Waiting list:	Usually 8-10 preparing to enter programs

Geographical Range — Areas Served

Although most clients are from the Tucson area, we receive statewide referrals from rural areas, especially those that have no alternatives for youth.

Staffing

Position	*Responsibilities*
Director of Independent Living Services	Oversee program services and budgets; Program development, staff training and development; Supervise staff, monitor cases, interview clients; Community liaison and community networking.
Case Manager	Interview potential clients, assess needs; Formulate individualized case plans with clients and parties relevant to the case and maintain

Case Manager (cont.)	ongoing correspondence with involved parties; Provide needs assessment, referral, and informal counseling through regular individual sessions; Assist clients with budgeting and money management; Supervise clients on a regular basis to support clients' application of daily living skills; Assist Director in community networking.
Outreach Worker	Educate community on homeless issues and services; Identify homeless youth eligible for services; Field referrals as initial point-of-entry for services; Work in conjunction with Peer Counselors in the community.
Life Skills Instructor	Facilitate classes and monitor behavior of group during speaker presentations; Develop and maintain the daily schedule of program; Determine and provide individual instruction to clients in special circumstances; Recruit, train, and supervise all volunteers; Generate and contact referrals, complete all paperwork, track attendance and progress; Assess clients' life skills through observation, pre-test, and post-test; Communicate information to relevant parties.
Peer Counselor	Conduct outreach for the agency by informing youth of services and programs; Co-facilitate groups and aftercare services; serve

Peer Counselor (cont.)
     as a positive role model;
Assist outreach worker and case managers with development and implementation of client goals;
Provide presentations and information to the community on a regular basis, both formally and informally.

Funding Sources

■ Per diem contracts with Department of Economic Security, Pima County Juvenile Court Center, Arizona Department of Juvenile Corrections, and other local youth providers

■ Health and Human Services (Outreach)

■ Housing and Urban Development - Pima County

■ City of Tucson contracts - Emergency Shelter Grant, City Development Block Grant, Title XX, Supportive Housing Program

Assessment of Client Strengths and Needs

We assess a client's strengths and needs through a variety of means. During the first contact, staff utilize a simple Immediate Needs Assessment (INA) to identify the youth's living situation, education and employment status, and basic needs. Through an interview, staff gain information on the youth's background, goals, and challenges. This enables us to gather basic requirements as well as get a basic understanding of his or her skills and experience level. The Life Skills Program utilizes a pre-assessment and final exam. Case management sessions offer ongoing opportunities to gather and document information in which identification of strengths and needs is emphasized.

> **Staff Comment**
>
> "Life Skills does give them the practical everyday tools, but this is not enough. Treating the students with respect and love helps them see and experience goodness. It also encourages them to bring forth their own courage, gentleness, perseverance, joy, contentment, peace of mind, and so on."

Life Skills Training Strategies

Life Skills Training is provided in several ways. The Life Skills Program is an 8-week course designed to teach the fundamentals of independent living. All youth are required to participate. Individual sessions can be arranged if there is a scheduling conflict or a client appears to need extra assistance. Youth are encouraged to use learned skills in their daily lives through case management support.

Client Involvement in Program Development

Clients are involved in program development through individual feedback, group discussions, and a client satisfaction survey. Client feedback is taken into consideration, and the program is designed to be flexible, so that adjustments for individual or group needs can be made.

Types of Housing Options Utilized by Open-Inn

TALP offers apartment housing for young adults ages 16½ to 18. Clients reside in shared two-bedroom apartments at a single site with 24-hour on-site staff presence. The CASA program utilizes the scattered-site apartment model, in which youth ages 18-21 select an apartment of their choice, based on appropriateness and convenience, and receive rent subsidy through the program. In addition, Open-Inn utilizes three studio apartments rented from the city of Tucson at a nominal cost. These units are commonly located and offered to independent living clients in need of more immediate housing or who don't qualify for scattered-site housing. Crisis shelter in a home-like setting is utilized for stabilization purposes for clients under age 18 seeking placement in independent living housing.

Staff Comment

"Working for Open-Inn's TALP program has had a positive effect on my life. Working with the teens as part of such a 'fine-tuned' team has upped my energy level and outlook on life."

Cost of Housing Options

Agency referrals are charged per diem for shelter and transitional services. Private (non-system) young adults can stay at shelter for no cost. Residents of TALP and CASA are charged a minimal program fee that doesn't exceed $50 per month.

Problems Specific to Each Option

- **TALP:**   The residential Houseparent sleeps at night, leaving the opportunity for residents to break rules;

  Parents or other involved parties whose involvement can interfere with client's ability to pursue goals;

  Single location can limit clients' choice of school and workplace;

  Location in Southeast Tucson in relation to public transportation can constrain clients' schedules and community access.

- **CASA:**   Scattered-site housing limits staff supervision of clients;
                     Lack of staff supervision enables clients with poor
                        household cleanliness;
                     Limited contact with staff makes communication
                        between client and Case Manager more difficult;
                     Lack of client interaction and peer support among clients.

Liability/Risk Management Issues

The program conducts intensive interviews and collects pertinent background information on referred youth prior to acceptance.   The Houseparent conducts random nighttime bed checks on minors in residence at TALP. Staff maintain communication with legal guardians and referral sources regarding clients' cases and share information regarding concerns and potential risks. Staff conduct daily apartment inspections at TALP and weekly apartment checks through CASA.

Staff address inappropriate client behavior in a timely manner, and clients are removed from the program for noncompliance when necessary. All clients sign an informed consent contract, consent to release information, agreement to confidentiality, and acknowledgment of client rights. Clients in CASA scattered-site housing sign their own leases. Open-Inn carries insurance against major problems.

Who Signs the Lease and Why?

Clients in CASA scattered-site housing sign their own leases in order to reduce agency liability, to enable them to continue residence in their apartments after exiting the program, and to allow them to build a positive rental history.

What Seems to be Working in Our Program and How Success is Measured

Life Skills Training has been consistently successful in providing useful information and decision-making practice for at-risk youth. Clients in independent living gain education and work experience through the program. Youth in the program have had to take responsibility for personal care — managing their time, cooking and cleaning for

> **Staff Comment**
>
> "You can't expect these kids to know better — they haven't had the so-called 'normal' experiences of growing up. You can't treat them like adults. You need to expect setbacks and a few failures, but with patience and consistency you'll see some of them learn and grow, and that's when you'll remember why you're here."

themselves, making appointments in the community — and in the process, they develop self-confidence. Allowing clients to experience the natural consequences of their actions has promoted resiliency.

Success in Life Skills Training is measured through a final exam. Tangible goal attainment, such as obtaining and maintaining employment, completing educational programs, and accumulating savings, comprises part of success evaluation. Success is also measured by evaluating clients' intangible skills, including their decision-making skills, self-awareness, and long-term planning.

Our Most Common Problems

1. Systems youth placed in TALP due to a lack of housing options often lack the commitment to program objectives necessary for success.

2. Youth who don't appreciate the opportunities being provided.

3. CASA Program is designed for youth who are neither employed nor attending public high school, so program requirements cannot always accommodate the demands of work or school in which a referred youth is participating.

4. Unhealthy relationships in clients' personal lives.

5. Lack of therapeutic counseling services available for youth.

6. Lack of adequate transitional and emergency shelter in the community to provide stabilization for young adults ages 18-21 prior to entry into independent living.

7. Lack of adequate mental and behavioral health supportive services for borderline clients.

8. College education programs selected through the Jackson Employment Center sometimes exceed the capacities of at-risk youth coming directly from disadvantaged situations.

9. High level of pregnancy and parenthood among referred population — parenting responsibilities sometimes interfere with successful maintenance of program responsibilities.

10. Youth often change their mind regarding their education after they are already underway.

Things Staff Would Like to See Happen

- On-site management for CASA housing.

- Stabilization shelter for 18-21 year olds.

- Contracted outpatient substance abuse treatment.

- More funding for supportive services (emergency assistance, utility assistance, supplies).

- Adjust CASA program guidelines to facilitate high school attendance and completion.

- Program staff are seeking to enhance the scattered-site housing program to make it easier for youth who attend traditional high school to participate in the program.

- Staff would like to develop a drop-in center offering services for basic needs to enhance outreach efforts.

- Programs in rural communities have developed more slowly than services in Tucson. Funding availability, competition with urban communities, and lack of community awareness have hampered rural development. However, progress has been made recently due to population growth and an increase in available funding.

Most Common Staff-Related Problems

1. Staff not taking initiative to address client issues as they arise.

2. Staff developing personal investment in clients' success.

3. Individualization of cases can lead to confusion regarding program protocol.

4. Scheduling case management sessions with busy clients.

Client Viewpoints

- Clients often express the desire to obtain program housing without the responsibilities of working, attending school, and budgeting finances.

- Clients often express the difficulty of handling the various program responsibilities, especially when these responsibilities are new to clients.

- Clients appear to lose interest in programming, especially in education, as they near program completion.

How Open-Inn Deals with Teen Parents

Open-Inn has two transitional housing programs that can accommodate teen parents ages 16-21 with children. We incorporate their needs as parents into their case plans. Through case management and referral, we ensure they obtain parenting support and education and health care, as well as government assistance and other services for which they are eligible. By providing housing and a support structure, we make it possible for many of our young parents who have neglected their education to return to school. Through Life Skills Training, we offer education and resources for prevention.

The teen parents Open-Inn works with face extraordinary challenges. Other services for families exist in the community, but teen parents often don't fit the mold for those programs because of their unique needs. Those young adults who have become parents are often those same at-risk and near-homeless youth struggling with a variety of issues, including juvenile delinquency; poor school performance; substance abuse; physical, sexual, and emotional abuse; mental and behavioral disorders; and family conflict. Often their parenthood is unplanned, resulting from poor decision making and a lack of preventive education and resources.

Many of these teen parents are surrounded by examples of unprepared parenthood among their peers and family, and they are often not the first generation of teen parents in their families. Most of our teen parents are young mothers, although many of the young men we work with have children living in the community. Our mothers commonly lack adequate support from the child's father and their families. Many of these young mothers express the perception that their child will fill an emotional void in their life. Some of these mothers are involved with the child welfare system and encounter the risk of losing custody of their children, based on their lack of stability, independence, and parenting skills. As parents, these teens must take on the adult responsibilities of parenting, employment, securing day care, obtaining health care, and household management.

Many of these at-risk teen parents are developmentally behind and have been unsuccessful in managing age-appropriate responsibilities. However, sometimes the enormous responsibility of a child can be transformative, providing an inspiration to be successful. Often, the teen parents we have worked with are committed to providing a life for their children that is healthier than the childhood they experienced. Cultivating this sense of hope and channeling it in a responsible direction is one of the challenging opportunities in working with teen parents.

10

Southern Nevada Independent Living Programs

Las Vegas, Nevada

Ken Meyer

Brief History

In the late 1980s, shortly after receiving federal IV-E-IL funding, Nevada began to address concerns about young adults aging out of foster care, thanks to the leadership of Dr. Thom Reilly. Nevada's share of the federal IV-E funds was about $120,000. The state hired two social workers, one for northern Nevada and one for southern Nevada. Their duties included:

1. Completing individual assessments of youth older than 15½;

2. Coordinating the development of written transitional plans;

3. Developing teen conferences with youth speak outs, i.e., youth advisory boards;

4. Developing a mentor program;

5. Providing life skills classes;

6. Training primary care providers;

7. Providing data for aftercare studies;

8. Locating affordable housing options;

9. Running job development workshops to locate employment with adequate income;

10. Seeking support from and educating the community.

One individual could not perform all of these duties. As a result, early community collaboration led to the establishment of the longest community partnership in state history with the Las Vegas Nevada Cooperative Extension office. The Las Vegas Nevada Cooperative Extension office is a branch of Nevada's land-grant college in Reno (UNR). During the 13-year collaboration, the Cooperative Extension has provided research-based instruction in life skills, with the mentor program, parenting program, delinquency reduction programs, and the development of a life plan portfolio by a Youth Specialist.

The in-kind match of services allowed Nevada to increase its share of the federal IV-E-IL dollars by some $30,000, to a yearly total of about $150,000, prior to the passage of the John C. Chaffee Independent Living Act of 1999. The Division of Child and Family Services worked to provide much of the independent living programming. Although this effort prevailed, it became evident that more help from the community would be required. A local foster care administrator suggested the development of a resource panel to review young adults' transitional plans and give constructive suggestions. The panel became known as the Teen Team. A local juvenile court judge called for the development of an independent living subcommittee to seek guidance and request services from community leaders. This community panel provides for significant community connections, especially with the school district.

Other than individualized efforts by primary care providers, no formal independent living program existed in the late 80s. The population of young adults aging out of care in southern Nevada remains today the same as then, about 100 per year. There are 271 young adults over age 15½ in foster care in southern Nevada. Of these, 36 are on the run, in a detention facility, or with parents. This remains relatively unchanging, despite a doubling of the Las Vegas population, which may be due to early intervention efforts (i.e., intensive family services) by the county. The county handles CPS investigations, and the state handles foster care. A representative of Stand up for Kids, a homeless drop-in center open 2 days per week, estimates that there are 150 homeless teens in Las Vegas. Of the 50 who use the drop-in center, 60% are local, and 40% are from out of town. In the early 90s, state-contracted providers began to respond to requests for independent living programs.

Working with Correctional Youth and Traditional Foster Youth

As a point of interest, both Nevada Homes and The Center for Independent Living wrote their contracts to provide out-of-home independent living preparation to parole and foster youth living together. Many new volunteers like CASAs and Mentors ask whether it is wise to house the two populations together. The Division and primary care providers have grown to accept this as an economic necessity. The argument is made that they have very similar backgrounds and that placement together is acceptable. However, The Center for Independent Living has drifted toward youth parolees, and Nevada Homes has drifted toward foster youth. The reason for this is not easy to pinpoint. Despite claims to the contrary, there is a quiet comfort with this split effort. Some foster youth have done fine in a population of predominantly youth parolees and vice versa. For independent living services, there needs to be a good assessment of the level of functioning of each youth when making recommendations for care. It seems to be the case in Nevada that the majority of foster youth are developmentally behind those in youth parole custody.

Contracted Primary Care Providers

Nevada Homes for Youth

Moore Enterprises Inc. is a residential group home care provider. Its founder, Ron Moore, MSW, recognized the need for transitional and independent living services in the population of young adults living in group-home care. He established a new enterprise called Nevada Homes for Youth to help young adults transition into our community. Nevada Homes for Youth began in the early 1990s with a 4-plex apartment near the corner of Maryland Parkway and Desert Inn in Las Vegas. It started as a coed facility, but soon it became a male-only facility. After years of learning from mistakes and concerns over drug use in the neighborhood, the facility closed. It was replaced by several scattered sites around Las Vegas.

The young adults liked these housing options (condominiums), but varying numbers of young adults made maintaining staff difficult. The numbers varied for a variety of reasons. To begin with, Nevada Homes sometimes took "meager referrals" (i.e., referrals not prepared for an IL placement), because they wanted to help the Division or a good social worker, or because they needed to increase their population. When meager referrals run into a roadblock like losing their job, most show confidence that they can find another, but it often takes longer than they think it will. This, of course, leads to loss of income and spending cash. If they are not in school, or if they're doing poorly in school, the young adults become vulnerable to promises of an easier time living with someone else (family member, friends, a family they found in the community, or a romantic interest). These options often turn out to be unrealistic. Helping young adults understand the stages of independence cannot always overcome their imagined bonds with family members. Usually by the time the youth realize this, they have already left the program and foster care. Nevada Homes built staff numbers to meet the population. However, when youth left unexpectedly, the program could not keep the new support staff. This was particularly painful when the support staff had the right stuff. Nevada state foster care workers typically have caseloads of about 45, so little supervision from the social worker could be provided. In 1 month, a program director could go from delegating work (such as transporting clients to the doctor) to doing it himself.

Description of Nevada Homes for Youth. With help from county/city grants dollars and a local business bank, the program recently remodeled a cement block building for administrative offices and dorm-style housing. Today, Moore Enterprises Inc. provides separate male and female transitional group homes, which are networked with apartment buildings owned and operated by Nevada Homes for Youth. The main housing location of Nevada Homes for Youth is two side-by-side four-unit, one-story apartment buildings for young adult women with on-site mentors. This main housing location is the priority placement, so the young adult women start here. This helps solve the challenge of a changing population. After showing responsibility in the main housing location, young adults can work toward scattered-site condos owned by Nevada Homes or choose their own place if they want to or are leaving foster care. Nevada Homes is the only scattered-site individual placement facility for youth in out-of-home care in Nevada. There is a scattered-site apartment building for males, but fewer males than females prove developmentally ready for the responsibility. Nevada Homes for Youth also provides options to parenting teens at its main housing location. The parenting teenager's child(ren) must be in the mother's custody for this option.

Program Services.

1. To provide primary care to young adults who will remain in out-of-home care until foster care ends at age 18, or until 19 if they are expected to complete high school or GED in that time.

2. To provide training in skills, knowledge, and information to function interdependently. This is accomplished on an individualized basis, unless the population is large enough to warrant group-style education.

3. To work with community-based organizations, including the Division of Child and Family Services (DCFS), to find and maintain employment with adequate income to live in the community.

4. To work with DCFS, Clark County School District, and Nevada Education Consultants to seek high school graduation and/or a GED. Note: Recently the school district began requiring students to pass proficiency tests in writing, reading, and math. This presents new roadblocks to graduation.

5. To help youth exit care with a reasonable plan, given the categorical age limits set by the state legislature.

Housing. The scattered-site apartments are owned by Nevada Homes for Youth. Each apartment is furnished with donated items and all basic supplies. In the past, phones with long distance blocks were provided, but the young adults found ways around the blocks, so phones are no longer supplied inside the apartments. Pay phones are available nearby. Sign-in sheets are used to help staff keep track of the young adults' whereabouts. Each young adult is expected to share an apartment with a peer. There is a one-bedroom condo available near the University of Nevada Las Vegas that can be earned. Typically, Nevada Homes owns the units, so landlords and leases are not dealt with. Rent for a two-bedroom apartment in the area around the Nevada Homes units ranges from $495 to $749.

Population. The population in apartments owned by Nevada Homes for Youth is primarily youth in DCFS custody, mostly from foster care and some from youth parole. The numbers vary from 10 to 25. A May 31, 2000 report shows 15 youth in DCFS care, placed in either Nevada Homes for Youth or Moore Enterprises. County probation and TANF (occasionally a young adult mother receiving TANF is placed with Nevada Homes) also utilize Nevada Homes for Youth for placement.   Referrals are received statewide. Agency-dependent, streetwise, and correctional youth bring different challenges to staff. Rules must be strictly enforced. A three-warnings system is used, with the youth's caseworker or parole officer notified at each warning. Nevada Homes can, by contract, demand a young adult's removal with a 10-day written notice. Nevada Homes uses site supervisors with an up-front, in-your-face style, but who can also back off as needed. No members of the opposite sex are allowed on the grounds, and overnights away from the main housing location must be cleared by DCFS. When a young adult moves out to a condo, there are fewer restrictions. Roommate relations and unwelcome or inappropriate visitors pose a constant challenge to staff in all apartment sites. Young adults who maintain employment with adequate income for 3 months can qualify to rent scattered-site units owned by Nevada Homes around the city for $450 per month after foster care ends. Most, both male and female, look to friends, family, and romantic interests to move on.

The Center for Independent Living

The Center for Independent Living, located on Las Vegas Boulevard, opened in the middle 90s. The principal contractors are Fred Gillis, Ph.D. and David Silverman, M.D. The housing consists of a three-story efficiency motel, converted into 30 studio apartments. The program started as coeducational, to provide an environment where learning independent living skills would be the focus, rather than controlling the environment. Within a year, the Center built a 4,000 square-foot office/recreational/multiple purpose room building to meet demand. Recently all young adult women transferred to two apartment buildings off site near the West Charleston Community College. One major challenge with coed facilities is dealing with promiscuous sexual behavior that stems from childhood sexual abuse. To help with this, males and females now live in separate buildings.

Description of The Center for Independent Living. Today, The Center for Independent Living has evolved into a facility where the young adult men and women reside at separate sites. Many of the young adult residents are parolees from the state youth correctional facilities in Elko and Caliente. Individuals age 16 to 19 years live in a structured, supportive, therapeutic environment where they can learn and develop independent living skills, while receiving specialized services to address each individual's emotional, behavioral, and vocational needs.

Program Services.

1. Housing: Each adolescent usually shares an apartment with one peer.

When space allows, youth can earn the right to live by themselves in an apartment. The apartments consist of a living room with a bunk bed, a bathroom with a tub and shower, and a fully equipped kitchen area with a refrigerator and convection/microwave oven.

2. Education: The Center believes in on-site educational opportunities. An Alternative Education School Counselor is contracted to see that individuals receive educational assessments including the following activities:

- Compile transcripts and tests from previous placements;

- Assess each student to determine a grade level in math, reading, and writing;

- Create an educational plan for the students to fill in educational gaps;

- Create a transition plan for the 18 to 19 year olds to enter a community college, trade school, vocational program, an apprenticeship program, or world of work;

- Train staff members to read and understand transcripts and Individual Educational Plans, know special education codes, and help students follow their academic plan;

- Help the student transition from one school district to another if that is appropriate to the academic plan.

3. Emotional support: Each youth is assigned a counselor, and all new arrivals attend support groups. Since some youth have family to return to, The Center acts as a transitional step back to their homes. A transitional support group, called "Project Magic," is facilitated by faculty from the Nevada Cooperative Extension.

4. Day Treatment: The Center provides intensive treatment to those young adults who require such service. An on-site Clinical Director works to see that young adults have a corrective emotional experience. This involves being in a consistent, supportive environment of their peers, where they will be treated in an adult fashion and where they will learn that their success is ultimately in their own hands.

Population. A May 31, 2000 report shows 15 youth receiving Medicaid from DCFS placed in The Center for Independent Living. Four young adults are in substitute care, while the remaining 11 are in youth parole. However, the population includes many who do not qualify for Medicaid. Capacity is close to 50. Referrals are received statewide.

Summary

Both programs have made many changes to meet the demands of preparing young adults for life after Division of Child and Family custody. An ongoing challenge is that our staff frequently take better paying jobs.

Good referrals remain in restrictive placements too long, both for good reasons (school, work, and positive relationships) and for bad reasons (high caseloads, worker turnover). Therefore, some poor referrals are made to these programs and often must be accepted. The staff, however, is hard working and has a "can do" attitude.

Other local agencies (like Boys Town, Regina Hall, Boulder City Children's Home, Sunrise Youth Services) and foster parents offer gradual steps to adult life. When primary care providers face the reality of this risky business, they struggle with state licensing requirements and liability concerns.

With reinforcements made possible by the John Chaffee program, state staff plans to lessen the abrupt end of services. Every bit of energy will be mustered to fight for approval of aftercare Medicaid coverage. In a state without income taxes, new costs are closely scrutinized. National agencies like NILA, National Resource Center, and Child Welfare League of America, as well as the federal government, are to be commended for their efforts in passing the John Chaffee program. In Nevada, the program is definitely helpful. I am optimistic that young adults aging out of care in Nevada will leave better prepared in the years to come with aftercare support.

A Success Story

Terry is now 21, working in an upscale department store in the cosmetics department and living with her longtime boyfriend in Las Vegas. She became a foster youth in 1985. Her mother and grandmother proved to be inadequate to the task of parenting Terry. Her father, whom she did not know, died when she was 13. The family her grandmother left her with used severe physical punishment.

Her first placement, which was in a single-parent foster home, did not meet her needs. Terry, a good student, dropped out of school and found work. At age 17, she was placed in a group home, since unfortunately there is a shortage of foster parents for teens in Nevada. While in the group home, Terry continued to work, save, and talk of completing a GED. Her birth family completely abandoned her. She had no adult support.

Terry wanted to live on her own. She thrived in the Nevada Homes Independent Living Program. Seldom home because of work, she always let staff know where she could be found. She purchased a pager and kept up the payments. She often talked about taking the GED but never got to it, perhaps because she knew that, if she passed the GED, foster care would end. She also knew that, without state support, she would likely move in with her boyfriend. Terry showed up for court review and managed to convince the agency to keep her case open until she reached age 19. That last year she received computer training and a new computer from Instructional Assess, a company the agency contracted with to improve young adults' employability.

After aging out, Terry completed her GED.

About the Contributors

Trevor Atwood has 3 years experience providing case management to at-risk youth in shelter, transitional living, independent living, and community corrections settings. Mr. Atwood chairs the Homeless Youth Committee of the Tucson Planning Council for the Homeless and works as a community advocate for the homeless. He is a trained volunteer facilitator in conflict resolution and community building workshops for youth and inmates. He participates in community activism and criminal justice reform efforts and serves as a board member with three local nonprofit groups: the Coalition of Arizonans to Abolish the Death Penalty, the Arizona American Friends Service Committee, and the Bodhisattva Institute, a Tibetan Buddhist dharma center. He has also worked as a writing consultant to college students. Mr. Atwood received degrees in Religion and Philosophy from the College of William and Mary in Virginia. Address: Open-Inn, 630 9th Street, Tucson, AZ 85705. Phone: 520-670-9040.

Darlene Dankowski, CBSW has served as the Executive Director of Open-Inn for the past 18 years. Her responsibilities include overseeing agency programs and budget, including grant writing and management liaison to the Board of Directors. Ms. Dankowski has a degree in Public Administration and extensive experience in directing shelter programs and services for runaway and homeless youth in Arizona. She has been a strong advocate for youth and is co-chair of the Children's Alliance Task Force on Homeless Children and Youth and a board member of the State Advisory Committee for Youth Development, Board President of the Tucson Preparatory School, Board member of the Arizona Council of Human Service Providers, Pima County Juvenile Court Incentive Grant Advisory Committee, Senate appointment to Child Services and is a Regional Peer Monitor for Region IX. Address: Open-Inn, 630 9th Street, Tucson, AZ 85705. Phone: 520-670-9040.

Meg Haffner has been with Youth Continuum, Inc. since 1994. She was Resident Advisor of UNO House from August 1994 to January 1997 and Acting Educational Coordinator during part of that time. She has been a CHAP Case Manager since January 1997 and a Therapeutic Crisis Intervention Trainer since October 1999. Prior to joining Youth Continuum, she spent 4 years as a child care worker and then assistant supervisor at St. Francis Home for Children in New Haven. She graduated from The University of Connecticut in 1990. Address: Youth Continuum, Inc., CHAP Program, 54 Meadow Street, 8th Floor, New Haven, CT 06519. Phone: 203-562-3396, extension 27.

Aldo Hurtado, MSW is the Director of the Latin American Youth Center's Transitional Living Program. A native of Nicaragua, Mr. Hurtado immigrated to the USA 14 years ago. He holds a bachelor's degree from the University of Maryland at College Park in Sociology and a master's in Social Work from the same institution. Mr. Hurtado has extensive experience working with families and adolescents of diverse backgrounds. His volunteer work and academic achievements have earned him several recognition awards in the field of Social Work. Address: Latin American Youth Center, 1419 Columbia Road, NW, Washington, D.C. 20009. Phone: 202-319-2292.

Mark J. Kroner, MSW, LSW is Director of the Division of Self-Sufficiency Services for Lighthouse Youth Services. He has also directed the scattered-site apartment Independent Living Program for Lighthouse since 1986. He has worked with over a thousand young people exiting the child welfare system. Mr. Kroner has worked in the field as a social worker, group home director, group trainer, and consultant. He has served on the National Independent Living Standards Committee of the Child Welfare League of America and the Ohio State Independent Living Task Force. He is a past president of the Ohio Independent Living Association. He has published numerous articles and workbooks focusing on self-sufficiency development. His latest book, *Housing Options for Independent Living Programs*, provides a summary of what is happening nationally related to housing youth leaving care. Mr. Kroner has spoken extensively around the country on independent living issues and has helped dozens of agencies start and develop scattered-site apartment programs. He testified before the House Ways and Means Subcommittee on Human Services concerning the Foster Care Independence Act of 1999 and was invited to attend the signing of the bill, where one of his program youth spoke on behalf of American foster youth. He received the National Independent Living Association Founders' Award in 2000. Address: Lighthouse Youth Services, Inc., 1501 Madison Road, Cincinnati, OH 45206. Phone: 513-487-7130.

Gerald P. Mallon, DSW is Assistant Professor and Chair of the Human Behavior sequence at the Hunter College School of Social Work in New York City. Dr. Mallon is the Founder of Green Chimneys programs for GLBTQ youth and author of several books about GLBTQ youth. In addition, he is the Chair of the Child Welfare League of America's Committee on the Revision of Standards for Independent Living. Address: Green Chimneys, 327 East 22nd, New York, NY 10010. Phone: 212-677-7288, extension 216.

Ken Meyer, MSW moved to Nevada in 1979 after receiving his BS in Business Administration from the University of Wisconsin-LaCrosse. He worked as a receiving manager and assistant product supervisor prior to joining the State of Nevada as a social worker. Initiated to social work as a case manager, Ken tentatively took the new position of Independent Living Consultant when created in 1987. Early work led to national recognition by the U. S. Department of Agriculture "Extension Review" for the Nevada Youth

Network consisting of Nevada Cooperative Extension, Nevada Business Services, and the Division of Child and Family Services. He brought to Nevada useful information attained while attending many international independent living conferences hosted by daniel, NILA, and National Resource Center. In 1997 he completed his MSW at the University of Nevada, Las Vegas. He was a co-presenter of "Mentoring Las Vegas Style" at the National Resource Center's independent living conference in San Antonio, Texas and Girls and Boys Town Professional Child Care Conference in 1998 at Boys Town, Nebraska. Address: Southern Nevada Independent Living Programs, 6171 West Charleston Blvd., Las Vegas, NV 89158. Phone: 702-486-6169.

Nancy Panico Lydic has been on the staff of Open-Inn since 1989. She has more than 9 years of experience working with older adolescents in out-of-home settings and has completed training in independent living services. She has been the Program Director of Open-Inn's Independent Living Services since 1995. Her responsibilities include overseeing the agency's statewide Independent Living programs and budgets, as well as direct management of the Pima County programs, including Street Outreach, Life Skills Training, Transitional Living, and Independent Living. She was responsible for the development and implementation of the scattered-site model of Independent Living for young adults. She represents Open-Inn on the Tucson Planning Council for the Homeless, and has been elected to the executive committee where she is currently the vice chair. She is a board member of the Tucson Preparatory School and represents Open-Inn on several committees focusing on homelessness. She is also a member of the TPCH subcommittees, The Homeless Young Adult Coalition, and the Continuum of Services committee. Ms. Panico has a degree in Sociology from the University of Arizona. Address: Open-Inn, 630 9th Street, Tucson, AZ 85705. Phone: 520-670-9040.

Denise Short has been employed at Youth Continuum, Inc. for 11 years, beginning as Group Home Senior Resident Advisor. She was later promoted to the position of CHAP Case Manager and, more recently, to CHAP Program Coordinator. Under Denise's leadership, the CHAP Program has serviced more youth than ever before, and more youth have successfully completed the programs. Also under Denise's leadership, the age limit in CHAP has been increased by 2 years, so that clients who started college or other post high school educational programs late now have the opportunity to remain in the program until they are 23 years old. Denise has actively participated in a number of workshops, including the National Independent Living, Regional Independent Living, Positive Youth Development, and Child Welfare League of America workshops. Outside of her secular work, Denise enjoys being educated through the Theocratic Ministry School in Orange, CT. Address: Youth Continuum, Inc., 54 Meadow Street, 8th Floor, New Haven, CT 06519. Phone: 203-562-3396, extension 26.

Jackie Smith, MSW, ACAC is the former Coordinator of the Community-Based Living Program at Spectrum Youth and Family Services. She is currently working at the Anna Marsh Behavioral Care Clinic based in Essex Junction, Vermont. She continues to be actively involved in independent living services within both her community and state, as well as nationally. Address: Anna Marsh Behavioral Care Clinic, 15 Pinecrest Drive, Essex Junction, VT 05452. Phone: 802-878-4399, extension 2005.

Diann E. Stevens, MS, LSW has been employed by Franklin County Children Services for 22 years. For the first 10 years she worked with children placed in foster homes, and for the last 12 years she has worked in the field of emancipation/independent living. She has been the Emancipation Department Director for the last 8 years. In addition, she is a board member of the National Independent Living Association. She served the NILA board as secretary for 2 years and is now the board vice-chairperson. Ms. Stevens is a past president of the Ohio Independent Living Association. She has also presented at many local, state, and national conferences dealing with independent living. Address: Franklin County Children Services, 1951 Gantz Road, Grove City, OH 43123. Phone: 614-278-5974.

Cheryl Tanis, MSW, LISW has been the Director of Quakerdale's New Providence Campus since 1988 and has worked in the field of social work since 1973, primarily for youth and family service agencies and programs. She supervises several programs, including family foster care and adoption services, residential treatment, family centered services, first offender community services, and scattered- and cluster-site independent living. She has served on several community boards and advisory groups, including The Home Connection School Youth Based Services and Visions for Health board chair, Hardin County Managed Care board member, Marshall County Youth and Violence Board, De-categorization advisory boards, The Coalition for Family and Children Services in Iowa family foster care and family centered committees, and the Providing Activities for Community Kids OJJDP board chair. Address: Quakerdale, Box 8, New Providence, IA 50206. Phone: 641-497-5276, extension 227.

Byron Wright has worked for Kenosha Human Development Services for 18 years and is currently the Executive Director. In the past, as coordinator of their transitional living programs, he developed and operated a scattered-site independent living program for 15 years. He also has run a scattered-site program for homeless youth for 9 years. (Both programs also have group home components.) Mr. Wright has consulted with other social service providers to help them establish similar programs. He has a BS from Florida State University. Address: Kenosha Human Development Services, 5407 8th Avenue, Kenosha, WI 53140. Phone: 414-657-7188.

Moving In

Ten Successful Independent/Transitional Living Programs

Poster Session

To Do:

- Assess community housing resources
- Line up funding sources
- Decide what options are affordable
- Develop rules and policies
- Train youth in self-sufficiency skills
- Train staff to teach IL skills
- Develop on-call & emergency procedures
- Anticipate problems & solutions
- Learn from other IL programs
- Address liability/licensing issues

The Causes:

- Familial poverty
- Death/illness
- Chemical dependency
- Mental illness
- Criminality
- Random misfortune
- Abuse/abandonment
- Lack of parenting skills
- Anti-family forces

Potential Problems:

- Drug/alcohol use
- Too many visitors/loud music
- Sexual activity
- Messy apartments
- Long-distance phone bills
- High utility bills
- Misuse of money
- Harboring minors/runaways
- Property damage
- Roommate arguments
- Lonely clients
- Time-management problems
- Negative peer pressure
- Self-sabotage
- Learned helplessness
- Lack of positive youth development

Desired Outcomes:

- Experience in living independently
- A chance to learn from mistakes
- A chance to understand the future
- A chance to live close to known supports
- Geographical flexibility
- No need to move again at discharge
- A chance to keep all furnishings
- A chance to develop coping skills
- A chance to increase self-awareness
- A chance to adjust to neighborhood

Appendix A

Independent Living Terminology*

1. AFTERCARE - Services/supports provided to youth following their discharge from the Child Protective service system. These services may be arranged prior to the youth's emancipation and may be free or based upon a fee.

2. ASSESSMENT CONFERENCE - A meeting between the client and the IL worker, with significant others sometimes in attendance, that determines the needs, strengths, limitations, and resources of a youth in an Independent Living Program.

3. CASE PLAN - The overall individualized plan for meeting the treatment and survival needs of a youth in county custody. The development of this plan is the responsibility of the county caseworker. It can also be called the Treatment Plan or Individualized Service Plan or Initial Service Plan.

4. CLUSTER-SITE APARTMENTS - Several apartments in a group. They can be owned by an agency or rented from a private landlord. In some cases, a staff member lives in one of the apartments or nearby. Sometimes referred to as supervised apartments.

5. CONTINUUM OF LIVING ARRANGEMENT OPTIONS - A variety of places where a youth who is preparing for emancipation can live, such as scattered-site apartments, host homes, mentor roommate apartments, boarding homes, shelters, shared homes, supervised apartments, and dorms. Youth may move from one type of living arrangement to another.

6. EMANCIPATION - The time when a child is released from child welfare custody, usually on his/her 18th birthday, but no later than his/her 21st birthday.

7. FEDERAL INDEPENDENT LIVING INITIATIVE - The Congressional act that amends Title IV-E of the Social Security Act to create funds for Independent Living Services. These funds cannot be used for room and board.

8. HARD SKILLS - Necessary, tangible self-sufficiency skills, such as money management, food and nutrition, community resources, and job skills.

9. HOST HOME - A living arrangement where an adult mentor or other responsible adult rents a room to a youth in his/her home. The living

arrangement could also be rented to an agency.

10. INDEPENDENCE - The state of being self-sufficient after emancipation from the child welfare system.

11. INDEPENDENT LIVING ASSESSMENT (ALSO REFERRED TO AS LIFE SKILL ASSESSMENT) - A formal assessment of a youth's skills as they relate to daily living activities. The assessment should evaluate "hard" skills, such as budgeting, cooking, banking, and health knowledge, as well as "soft" skills, such as time management, assertiveness, decision making, and problem solving. The assessment tool varies from county to county. Some counties or agencies develop and use their own assessments. Others purchase copyrighted assessment tools.

12. INDEPENDENT LIVING PLAN - A plan developed as part of the youth's overall case plan that outlines steps to be taken to prepare a youth without stable family support for life after the child welfare system.

13. LIFE BOOK - A documented history of a youth's life, including pictures, certificates, lists of placements, schools, health care, etc. for the youth to keep.

14. LIFE SKILLS CURRICULUM - A course of study to teach the hard and soft skills in the 16 areas identified by the State of Ohio.

15. LIFE SKILLS/SELF-SUFFICIENCY TRAINING - Training in hard and soft skills that everyone needs to function as a responsible, independent adult in the community.

16. MENTOR - Someone, usually over the age of 21, who acts as a supportive role model for a vulnerable or at-risk youth. Mentors can be volunteers, students, paid adults, former clients, etc.

17. MENTOR APARTMENT - An apartment rented to a youth with a mentor roommate, who is usually over 21.

18. PRE-INDEPENDENT LIVING - Any prior type of training or experience related to preparing a youth to live on his/her own. Sometimes called self-sufficiency training.

19. SCATTERED-SITE APARTMENT - An individual apartment, usually rented from a private landlord, that can be located anywhere in a community.

20. SHARED HOME/SHARED LIVING - A living arrangement where a youth shares a home with other youth and minimal adult supervision. In some cases, the supervision is the home; in others, it is not.

21. SOFT SKILLS - Necessary, intangible self-sufficiency skills, such as social skills, time management, communication, and anger management.

22. STATE INDEPENDENT LIVING COORDINATOR - Individual designated to oversee ODHS Independent Living Programs and to ensure the guidelines are followed. The Coordinator acts as a liaison between counties and ODHS and advocates for the counties' needs.

23. SINGLE ROOM OCCUPANCY (SRO) - Housing that generally is less expensive than renting an apartment. Tenants share in using the kitchen, living room, etc. Each tenant is provided with his/her own bedroom.

24. STIPEND - A payment to a youth for performance of a specific responsibility.

25. TRANSITIONAL LIVING/SEMI INDEPENDENT LIVING/SUPERVISED INDEPENDENT LIVING PROGRAM - In general, TL means any type of living arrangement that helps a youth learn skills needed for the next, less supervised setting. Some campus programs have assigned a house to serve as a transitional living experience before a youth leaves the system and moves out on his/her own. Some agencies refer to TL as housing-based services for older homeless youth and young adults who are not in the system. It is best to ask anyone who says they have a TL program to define it in their terms. These are usually supervised by an adult who lives in or near the living arrangements of the youth.

26. YOUTH CONFERENCES/TRAININGS - Meetings, usually a full day or longer, which bring together youth in Independent Living (IL) to learn and share IL skills. Recreation may be a part of these conferences.

*This list was compiled by the Southern Ohio Independent Living Association, 1999. *Independent Living* is used synonymously with *self-sufficiency*.

Appendix B

Assessing Local Resources for Developing Independent Living Services

Questions to guide your discussion:

1. Who makes the decisions concerning placement of older teens in this community?

2. What are you doing now with older teens who will be aging out of the system?

3. Are the key people in this community aware of different arrangement options that are being used to prepare youth for independent living?

4. Are there available, affordable apartments in this community that are in safe, convenient neighborhoods?

5. Are there landlords who would be willing to rent to a youth living alone at 18? 17? 16½?

6. Are there significant numbers of youth who could benefit from different independent living arrangements? Can you get statistics to support your case?

7. Who would be in the best position to start and run such a program?

   the local public children's services agency?   _____

   a private non-profit subcontractor?   _____

8. Are there staff in existing programs who could start working with one or several youths in an apartment setting while still fulfilling their other functions?

9. Are there local people who would be willing to rent a room in their homes to a teen under agreed-upon terms?

10. If apartments are available, can they be equipped with donated furnishings from local church groups, civic clubs, agency friends, etc.?

11. Can the program find volunteers to provide support, life-skills training, client-supervision, etc.?

Is there a school that could provide student interns to work in an ILP?

12. Can someone in the community donate a building for such a purpose? (city council, church group, foundation, private donors, HUD?)

13. Are there local, state, or federal grants available to buy property for such a purpose?

14. Are there local foundations that would assist in developing such a program?

15. If a building is available (e.g., for a shared home or supervised apartment program), can anyone assist in rehabbing, painting, furnishing it? (volunteers, fraternities, civic clubs, school or university groups, corporate groups)?

16. Can the agency lease an already-rehabbed building, old motel, or under-utilized SRO for independent living preparation?

17. Could a local agency board start fund-raising efforts to raise money for such an endeavor?

18. Are there licensing or zoning rules that hinder the development of the less restrictive living arrangement options such as scattered-site apartments?

19. Is there anything you can do now to assist this state in developing licensing standards that open up new possibilities? (organize a meeting, write letters, volunteer to coordinate group, etc.?)

20. Has the liability issue been resolved concerning placing youth in their own semi-supervised apartments?

21. What else could be done to improve emancipation services for our teens?

Appendix C

Comparing Housing Options Variables

	Supervised Apartments	Shared Homes	Scattered-Site Apartments	Roommate Apartments	Host Homes	Boarding Homes	Subsidized Housing	Dorm
Purchase Property								
Rehabilitation Costs								
Security Deposit								
Monthly Rent								
Furnishings								
Supplies								
Utilities								
Phone								
Maintenance								
Repairs								
Live-In Staff								
24-hour Staff Coverage								
Overnight Staff								
Move Again at Discharge								
Misc./Hidden Expenses								
Insurance								

Appendix D

Rating Your Current Independent Living Efforts

Rate your current independent living efforts with the following scale:

1.____We have a state mandate to provide independent living services. (5 points)

2.____We have a full-time person in our agency assigned to ILP development. (5 points) (part-time person = 3 points)

3.____Our agency has completed staff training re: independent living issues. (5 points)

4.____We have read materials on other independent living programs around the country. (3 points)

5.____Key members of our community's children's services system have met to discuss needs for IL services for our teens. (3 points)

6.____We have already started assessing the overall level of IL functioning of the youth 15 and older in our community. (2 points)

7.____We have started life skills training classes. (3 points) (over 6 months of classes = 5 points)

8.____We have an IL workbook or curriculum that we use regularly with our teens. (3 points)

9.____We start IL/self-sufficiency preparation with our teens before they are 16 years old. (4 points)

10.____Our community foster parents/social workers receive training on how to prepare their teens for independent living. (3 points)

11.____Our community caseworkers/social workers/child care workers have received training on IL living arrangement options. (3 points)

12.____Our state has licensing that allows for real-life IL experience and semi-supervised IL living arrangement options. (4 points)

13.____Our community has a supervised apartment program for independent living preparation. (5 points)

14.____Our community has a scattered-site apartment program. (5 points)

15.____Our community has other available living arrangements for teens leaving the child welfare system. (5 points)

16.____Our teens are able to keep their living arrangements after they are out of custody. (5 points)

17.____Our community includes independent living preparation in the overall client case plan. (3 points)

18.____Our community children's services leaders have been educated about new living arrangement options. (3 points)

19.____Our juvenile court system is supportive of experiential/semi-supervised independent living preparation programs. (4 points)

20.____We have access to donated items (furniture, supplies) for our teens who are leaving the system. (3 points)

21.____We have a full-time independent living program in our community that coordinates all IL services. (7 points)

22.____We have good cooperation between the public and private sectors concerning IL program development. (5 points)

23.____We have obtained long-term funding sources for our independent living program. (9 points)

24.____Our community has a continuum of independent living arrangement options for teens leaving the system. (9 points)

25.____We are fairly well networked with other IL programs around the country. (4 points)

26.____We have received title IV-E funds for IL preparation. (5 points)

27.____We have received HUD/transitional living funds for our community. (5 points)

28.____We utilize mentors, students, and/or volunteers to help our teens get ready for independent living. (5 points)

29.____We have a means to track our youth after they leave care. (5 points)

30.____Our staff understand the state guidelines for ILP. (5 points)

Other areas of your program that you think deserve "points" (on a scale of 1-5):

_____ (____points)

_____ (____points)

total score = _____

Mark J. Kroner 1998

Appendix E

What It Takes to Develop and Run
Successful Independent Living Services

1. Time and patience

2. A shifting of resources

3. Public/private partnerships

4. Changes in the state code

5. Case-by-case program development

6. Tolerance of mistakes — client and program

7. Extra money to cover damages and hidden costs

8. Getting the entire system involved

9. A countywide self-sufficiency program

10. Giving youth many chances

Appendix F

Resources for Independent and Transitional Living

Suggested Readings: Journal Articles

Barth, R. P. (1990). On their own: The experiences of youth after foster care. *Child and Adolescent Social Work, 7* (5), 419-440.

Boyle, P. (2000). Young advocates sway Washington: Odd fellows team scores $70 million hike for independent living. *Youth Today, 9* (2), 1, 52-57.

Brinkman, A. S., Dey, S., & Cuthbert, P. (1991). A supervised independent-living orientation program for adolescents. *Child Welfare, 70* (1), 69-80.

Cook, R. (1994). Are we helping foster care youth prepare for their future? Special issue: Preparing foster youth for adulthood. *Children and Youth Services Review, 16* (3-4), 213-229.

Courtney, M. E., & Barth, R. P. (1996). Pathways of older adolescents out of foster care: Implications for independent living services. *Social Work, 41* (1), 75-83.

Davis, M., & Vander Stoep, A. (1997). The transition to adulthood for youth who have serious emotional disturbance: Developmental transition and young adult outcomes. *The Journal of Mental Health Administration, 24* (4), 400-427.

English, D. J., Kouidou-Giles, S., & Plocke, M. (1994). Readiness for independence: A study of youth in foster care. Special issue: Preparing foster youth for adulthood. *Children and Youth Services Review, 16* (3-4), 147-158.

First, R. J., Rife, J. C., & Toomey, B. G. (1994). Homelessness in rural areas: Causes, patterns and trends. *Social Work, 39,* 97-108.

Goerge, R., Wulczyn, F., & Fanshel, D. (1994). A foster care research agenda for the '90s. *Child Welfare, 73* (5), 525-552.

Hahn, A. (1994). The use of assessment procedures in foster care to evaluate readiness for independent living. Special issue: Preparing foster youth for adulthood. *Children and Youth Services Review,* 16 (3-4), 171-179.

Iglehart, A. P. (1994). Adolescents in foster care: Predicting readiness for independent living. Special issue: Preparing foster youth for adulthood. *Children and Youth Services Review, 16* (3-4), 159-169.

Kroner, M. J. (1988a). Living arrangement options for young people preparing for independent living. *Child Welfare, 67* (6), 547-562.

Kroner, M. J. (1988b). The role of foster parents in the preparation of youth for independent living: One agency's observations. New Life Youth Services, Cincinnati, Ohio. *Daily Living, 8* (3), 6-8.

Kroner, M. J. (1989). A day in the life of the New Life Independent Living Program. *Daily Living, 8* (1), 8.

Kroner, M. J. (1993). Defining success: One client at a time. *Daily Living, 7* (4), 8, 12.

Kroner, M. J. (1997). Ten years later: Reflections on running an independent living program. *Daily Living, 11* (2), 2-4.

Kroner, M. J. (1999). Another day in the life of an independent living program. *Daily Living, 13* (1), 6-7.

Mallon, G. P. (1992). Junior life skills: An innovation for latency age children in out-of-home care. *Child Welfare, 71* (6), 585-591.

Mallon, G. P. (1998). After care, then where? Outcomes of an independent living program. *Child Welfare, 77* (1), 61-78.

Mangine, S. J., Royse, D., Wiehe, V. R., & Nietzel, M. T. (1990). Homelessness among adults raised as foster children: A survey of drop-in center users. *Psychological Reports, 67,* 739-745.

McMillen, J. C. (1999). Better for it: How people benefit from adversity. *Social Work, 44* (5), 455-468.

McMillen, J. C., & Tucker, J. (1999). The status of older adolescents at exit from out-of-home care. *Child Welfare, 78* (3), 339-360.

Mech, E. V. (1994). Foster youths in transition: Research perspectives on preparation for independent living. *Child Welfare, 73* (5), 603-623.

Mech, E. V., & Fung, C. C.-M. (1999). Placement restrictiveness and educational achievement among emancipated foster youth. *Research on Social Work Practice, 9* (2), 213-228.

Mech, E. V., Ludy-Dobson, C., & Hulseman, F. (1994). Life skills knowledge: A survey of foster adolescents in three placement settings. Special issue: Preparing foster youth for adulthood. *Children and Youth Services Review, 16* (3-4), 181-200.

Mech, E. V., Pryde, J. A., & Rycraft, J. R. (1995). Mentors for adolescents in foster care. *Child and Adolescent Social Work Journal, 12* (4), 317-328.

Nixon, R. (1997). Introduction. *Child Welfare, 76* (5), 571-576.

Nollan, K. A., Wolf, M., Ansell, D., Burns, J., Barr, L., Copeland, W., & Paddock, G. (2000). Ready or not: Assessing youths' preparedness for independent living. *Child Welfare, 79* (2), 159-176.

Oden, S. (1995). Studying youth programs to assess influences on youth development: New roles for researchers. Special issue: Creating supportive communities for adolescent development. *Journal of Adolescent Research, 10* (1), 173-186.

Roman, N. P., & Wolfe, P. B. (1997, winter). The relationship between foster care and homelessness. *Public Welfare,* 4-9.

Scannapieco, M., Schagrin, J., & Scannapieco, T. (1995). Independent living programs: Do they make a difference? *Child and Adolescent Social Work Journal, 12* (5), 381-389.

Vissing, Y. M., & Diament, J. (1997). Housing distress among high school students. *Social Work, 42* (1), 31-41.

Waldinger, G., & Furman, W. M. (1994). Two models of preparing foster youths for emancipation. Special issue: Preparing foster youth for adulthood. *Children and Youth Services Review, 16* (3-4), 201-212.

Suggested Readings: Books and Reports

*Available from LotsofLearning.com

Burrell, K., & Perez-Ferreiro, V. (1995). *A national review of management of the federally funded Independent Living Program.* Washington, DC: U.S. Department of Health and Human Services.

Clark, H. B., & Davis, M. (Eds.). (2000). *Transition to adulthood: A resource for assisting young people with emotional or behavioral difficulties.* Baltimore, MD: Brookes Publishing Co.

Cook, R. (1991). *A national evaluation of Title IV-E foster care independent living programs for youth. Phase 2: Final report.* Rockville, MD: Westat, Inc.

Courtney, M. E., Piliavin, I., & Grogan-Taylor, A. (1995). *The Wisconsin study of youth aging out of out-of-home care: A portrait of children about to leave care.* Madison, WI: Institute for Research on Poverty. Retrieved September 12, 2000 from the World Wide Web: http://polyglot.lss.wisc.edu/socwork/foster/fcreport.html

Homelessness: Programs and the people they serve - highlights report. Retrieved December 21, 1999 from the World Wide Web: http://www.huduser.org/publications/homeless/homelessness/highrpt.html

*Kroner, M. J. (1999). *Housing options for independent living programs.* Annapolis Junction, MD: CWLA Press.

*Mech, E. V., & Rycraft, J. R. (1995). *Preparing foster youths for adult living: Proceedings of an invitational research conference.* Washington, DC: Child Welfare League of America.

Rutter, M. (1990). Psychological resilience and protective mechanisms. In J. Rolf, A. S. Masten, D. Chichetti, K. H. Neuchterlein, & S. Weintraub (Eds.), *Risk and protective factors in the development of psychopathology* (pp. 181-214). New York: Cambridge University Press.

*Stone, H. D. (1987). *Ready set go: An agency guide to independent living.* Washington, DC: Child Welfare League of America.

Westat, Inc. (1988). *A national evaluation of Title IV-E foster care independent living programs for youth. Final report.* Washington, DC: U.S. Department of Health and Human Services.

Suppliers of Resources for
Independent and Transitional Living

Lots of Learning.com
Northwest Media, Inc.
(catalog and Web site of IL-focused resources, videos, books)
326 West 12th Avenue
Eugene, OR 97401
800/777-6636
FAX: 541/343-0177
E-mail: nwm@northwestmedia.com
http://www.lotsoflearning.com

Boys Town Press
(catalog of resources for youth-serving professionals, educators, and parents)
14100 Crawford Street
Boys Town, NE 68010
800/282-6657
FAX: 402/498-1310
E-mail: BTPress@boystown.org
http://www.boystown.org/products/booksvideos/btpress.htm

The Bureau For At-Risk Youth
(catalog of resources for at-risk youth)
135 Dupont Street
P.O. Box 760
Plainville, NY 11803-0760
800/99-YOUTH
FAX: 516/349-5521
E-mail: info@at-risk.com
http://www.at-risk.com

Child Welfare League of America
(training and consulting, resource catalog)
440 First Street NW, Third Floor
Washington, DC 20001-2085
202/638-2952
FAX: 202/638-4004
http://www.cwla.org

daniel
(IL conferences, training, and resources catalog)
4203 Southpoint Boulevard
Jacksonville, FL 32216
800/226-7612
FAX: 904/296-1953
E-mail: info@danielkids.org
http://www.danielmemorial.org

Independent Living Resources, Inc.
(IL resources catalog, training, and consulting)
411 Andrews Road, Suite 230
Durham, NC 27705
800/820-0001
FAX: 919/384-0338
E-mail: ilrinc@mindspring.com
http://www.ilrinc.com

Kids Rights
(catalog of resources)
8902 Otis Avenue
Indianapolis, IN 46216
800/892-KIDS (5437)
FAX: 877/543-7001
E-mail: kidsrights@jist.com
http://www.kidsrights.com

Lighthouse Youth Services, Inc.
(IL resources)
1501 Madison Road, Second Floor
Cincinnati, OH 45206
513/487-7130
http://www.mkroner@lys.org

National Resource Center for Youth Services
(youth resource catalog, training and consulting, IL conferences)
The University of Oklahoma College of Continuing Education
4502 East 41st Street
Tulsa, OK 74135-2553
918/660-3700
FAX: 918/660-3737
E-mail: rbaker@ou.edu
http://www.nrcys.ou.edu

School-to-Work
(resource catalog)
P.O. Box 9
Calhoun, KY 42327-0009
800/962-6662
http://www.nimcoinc.com

Sunburst Technology
(adolescent resources catalog)
101 Castleton Street
Pleasantville, NY 10570
800/431-1934
FAX: 914/747-4109
http://www.sunburst.com

Wisconsin Clearinghouse for Prevention Resources
(resource catalog)
University Health Services
University of Wisconsin-Madison
Dept. 7B
P.O. Box 1468
Madison, WI 53701-1468
800/322-1468
FAX: 608/262-6346
http://www.uhs.wisc.edu/wch

Organizations

Casey Family Programs
1300 Dexter Avenue North
Seattle, WA 98109-3547
206/282-7300
FAX: 206/282-3555
http://www.casey.org

Child Welfare League of America
440 First Street NW, Third Floor
Washington, DC 20001-2085
202/638-2952
FAX: 202/638-4004
http://www.cwla.org

National Foster Parent Association
P.O. Box 81
Alpha, OH 45301-0081
800/557-5238
FAX: 937/431-9377
E-mail: nfpa@donet.com
http://www.nfpainc.org

National Independent Living Association
4203 Southpoint Boulevard
Jacksonville, FL 32216
800/226-7612
FAX: 904/296-1953
E-mail: info@nilausa.org
http://www.nilausa.org

Web Sites: Northwest Media

www.lotsoflearning.com
Northwest Media's secure online shopping center
for quality social learning products

www.echeckin.com
An Internet-based support program for youth in
Independent Living/Life Skills programs

www.northwestmedia.com
Northwest Media, Inc.
Resources

Web Sites: Other

www.acf.dhhs.gov
The Administration for Children and Families
Legislation, National Developments

www.casey.org
Casey Family Programs
Resources

www.cwla.org
Child Welfare League of America
Resources, Advocacy, Training, Conferences

www.connectforkids.org
Connect for Kids
Articles on Child Welfare and Youth Work

www.ncfy.com
National Clearinghouse on Families & Youth
Resources on Youth and Family Policy and Practice

www.nfpainc.org
National Foster Parent Association
Resources

www.nilausa.org
National Independent Living Association
Advocacy, National and Regional IL Information

www.nrcys.ou.edu
National Resource Center for Youth Services
Resources, Training, Conferences

www.orphan.org
The Orphan Foundation of America
Scholarships for Former Foster Youth, IL Resources, Resources

COMMENTS

Send your comments to: Northwest Media, Inc.
326 West 12th Ave., Eugene, OR 97401
e-mail: nwm@northwestmedia.com